Presented to

_____

On the occasion of

_____

From

_____

Date

_____

© 2000 by Barbour Publishing, Inc.

ISBN 1-57748-765-6

Unless otherwise noted, all Scripture quotations are taken from the King James Version of the Bible.

Scripture quotations marked (NIV) are taken from the HOLY BIBLE: NEW INTERNATIONAL VERSION®, NIV®, copyright © 1973, 1978, 1984 by International Bible Society. Used by permission of Zondervan Publishing House. All rights reserved.

Scripture quotations marked (NLT) are taken from the *Holy Bible,* New Living Translation, copyright © 1996. Used by permission of Tyndale House Publishers, Inc., Wheaton, Illinois 60189, U.S.A. All rights reserved.

Scripture quotations marked (NASB) are taken from the NEW AMERICAN STANDARD BIBLE®, © Copyright The Lockman Foundation 1960, 1962, 1963, 1968, 1971, 1972, 1973, 1975, 1977. Used by permission.

Published by Barbour Publishing, Inc., P.O. Box 719, Uhrichsville, Ohio 44683 http://www.barbourbooks.com

ecpa Member of the
Evangelical Christian
Publishers Association

Printed in the United States of America.

GOD'S WORD FOR

Women

HUMBLECREEK

INSPIRATION FOR LIFE

INTRODUCTION

Though it was written thousands of years ago, God's Word has much to say to the modern woman. The Bible addresses the important issues that women face: family, jobs, self-image, the meaning of life. When carefully read and pondered, the Bible provides the answers to the deepest questions women have.

Over the years, many godly women have unlocked important Bible passages—and then written their insights for the benefit of others. That's what *God's Word for Women* is all about—sharing the knowledge that the Bible offers to all. This collection of more than 180 devotionals, a full six months' worth, will challenge you in your spiritual life, providing the insights you need to find wholeness in God, through His Son Jesus Christ.

You'll find a rich variety of writings in *God's Word for Women*. Some devotionals date back to the 1800s, while others were written at the close of the twentieth century. All offer an important insight into God's Word, and the issues of your life.

When a book title follows a passage, that book is available through many Christian bookstores from Barbour Publishing, Inc. Many of those devotionals which are not so labeled, and others like them, can be found in the book *A Gentle Spirit,* also published by Barbour Publishing. If you find these selections helpful, you may want to pursue further reading in these sources.

May God bless your spiritual journey as you read *God's Word for Women.*

A Blessed New Year

But the land. . .is a land. . .which the LORD thy God careth for:
the eyes of the LORD thy God are always upon it, from the
beginning of the year even unto the end of the year.
DEUTERONOMY 11:11–12

Today, dear friends, we stand upon the verge of the un-known. There lies before us the new year and we are going forth to possess it. Who can tell what we shall find? What new experiences, what changes shall come, what new needs shall arise? But here is the cheering, comforting, gladdening message from our heavenly Father, *"The LORD thy God careth for it."* *"His eyes are upon it away to the ending of the year."*

If He be the Source of our mercies, they can never fail us. No heat, no drought can parch that river, "the streams where-of make glad the city of God."

The land is a land of *hills* and *valleys.* It is not all smooth nor all downhill. If life were all one dead level, the dull same-ness would oppress us; we want the hills and the valleys. The hills collect the rain for a hundred fruitful valleys. Ah, so it is with us! It is the hill difficulty that drives us to the throne of grace and brings down the shower of blessing; the hills, the bleak hills of life that we wonder at and perhaps grumble at, bring down the showers.

We cannot tell what loss and sorrow and trial are doing. Trust only. The Father comes near to take our hand and lead us on our way today. It shall be a good, a blessed new year!

from *Streams in the Desert*
by MRS. CHARLES E. COWMAN

BE STILL

Be still, and know that I am God:
I will be exalted among the heathen,
I will be exalted in the earth.

PSALM 46:10

Another morning, the persistent chirp of a mother robin outside our bedroom window awakened me. I glanced at the clock. 4:30 A.M. *How can birds be awake so early?* I wondered.

I found myself alert, as though a quiet voice were beckoning me to our backyard patio. I slipped on my robe, tiptoed to the kitchen, and quietly prepared a cup of hot tea. The crisp, gentle breeze caressed my cheeks when I pushed back the sliding glass door. I settled into my favorite patio chair—just me, my cup of tea, and best of all, my Lord.

"Be still and know that I am God," I felt Him whisper on the wind.

I knew I would soon be challenged with endless responsibilities in the next few days. I had already asked for His help. In the solitude of a backyard heavenly chapel, the Lord and I shared secrets, concerns, and direction for an hour and a half. I thought I would be tired. Instead, I felt exhilarated by His Spirit.

I frequently return to my favorite spot while the whole world sleeps. There I regain the strength and guidance He always has to give.

Give ear to my words, O LORD, consider my meditation. . . .
My voice shalt thou hear in the morning, O LORD;
in the morning will I direct my prayer unto thee,
and will look up.

PSALM 5:1, 3

from *When I'm on My Knees*
by ANITA CORRINE DONIHUE

WAIT LIKE THE EAGLE

But they that wait upon the LORD shall renew their strength;
they shall mount up with wings as eagles; they shall run, and
not be weary; and they shall walk, and not faint.

ISAIAH 40:31

Waiting is one of the hardest things to do, especially when the years go by and our dreams and plans have not yet been fulfilled. Indeed, we spend much of our lives waiting for direction.

The *American Heritage Dictionary* offers this definition of *wait:*

"To remain inactive or stay in one spot until something anticipated occurs or to be in a state of readiness." Surely that describes the eagle, for it knows how to wait in many situations.

The eagle will perch on a rock waiting for the sun to rise and the wind to make thermal currents. While the eagle waits, it looks down to the ground to see if there is any prey. When it spots its prey, the eagle usually chooses to wait. Then, at the right moment, it swoops down.

Before we mount up on wings like eagles, we must learn to wait.
That was a lesson for the children of Israel who were told to wait for the cloud to guide them by day. They had to move when the cloud moved and wait when the cloud stopped.

Like the Old Testament Hebrews, occasionally we are told to wait in the midst of trials or heartache as "the cloud" disappears. Waiting can be for a few minutes or for many years.

Then there are times when we feel comfortable and settled into a place and we notice the cloud begins to move. When we move as God's hand guides us, safely under His wings, we will soar to new places and heights.

from *Soar As the Eagle*
by SHERYL LYNN HILL

A Deeper Meaning

I will open my mouth in a parable:
I will utter dark sayings of old.
PSALM 78:2

S arah, the old woman with mysteries to tell. The whole
town buzzed around Sarah's house. Sarah had lived in the
same house in the same town for seventy years. She was a
throwback to an earlier time. She dressed in fashions of the
twenties, and she talked a language that sounded foreign to
young ears. Sarah was a walking cliché. She remembered the
stories and sayings of old, and so she was a treasure chest of
days gone by. Everyone loved Sarah, for Sarah was history
come to life.

Life is a story. It is a parable we live through day by day.
Just as a parable has a hidden meaning, so, too, the events of
our daily living have significance and deeper meanings. Our
present and our past are important components of who we
are. We like to hold onto the past, and we strive to make the
present the best it can be. God, the greatest storyteller of all,
is a part of our past and our present. He can shape our parable for us, if we will let Him. When we do so, we can be confident that our story will have a happy ending.

∞

I don't have any idea what the outcome of my story will be, Lord,
but I thank You for giving my life an interesting and unique plot.
Go with me through the chapters of my life, Lord. Amen.

from *Wisdom from the Psalms*

GOD CARES

Therefore take no thought, saying,
What shall we eat? or, What shall we drink?
or, Wherewithal shall we be clothed?
... for your heavenly Father knoweth that
ye have need of all these things.
MATTHEW 6:31–32

Who is the best cared for in every household? Is it not the little children? And does not the least of all, the helpless baby, receive the largest share? We all know that the baby toils not, neither does it spin; and yet it is fed, and clothed, and loved, and rejoiced in more tenderly than the hardest worker of them all.

This life of faith, then, consists in just this—being a child in the Father's house. And when this is said, enough is said to transform every weary, burdened life into one of blessedness and rest.

Let the ways of childish confidence and freedom from care, which so please you and win your heart in your own little ones, teach you what should be your ways with God; and, leaving yourself in His hands, learn to be literally "careful for nothing"; and you shall find it to be a fact that the peace of God, which passeth all understanding, shall keep (as with a garrison) your heart and mind through Christ Jesus.

from *The Christian's Secret of a Happy Life*
by HANNAH WHITALL SMITH

PRAISE HIM IN SONG

Take a psalm,
and bring hither the timbrel,
the pleasant harp with the psaltery.
PSALM 81:2

Beth was different when she was singing. Somehow the pressures of the world disappeared when the music filled her head and heart. Her whole life felt somehow lighter, brighter, when she lifted her voice in praise through song. Music was the best expression of who she was and what she believed. Music made God real to Beth.

Music is a universal language. Every culture has its music, and it is revered as one of the finest arts. Music brings people together and can move us closer to God. God loves music and the spirit from which music springs. The quality is not nearly as important as the intention of the heart. Sing out to God, and He will bless you richly.

∽∞

Music touches my heart in a special way, Lord. Speak to me through the beauty of music. Touch me day by day. Amen.

from *Wisdom from the Psalms*

THE UNEXPECTED

For I know the thoughts that I think toward you,
saith the LORD, thoughts of peace,
and not of evil, to give you an expected end.
JEREMIAH 29:11

Anne breathed in the sweet smell of powder mixed with clean baby. She gave the soft, round bottom a quick pat before she fastened her new daughter's diaper. She snuggled the baby close, reveling in motherhood. Her joy dimmed only a moment at the thought which had haunted her the entire nine months of her pregnancy. How could a mother give up her little child? Anne's mother had done just that: She had left her husband and then three-year-old Anne to find a life of "fun," so the story went.

"I'll never abandon you, little one," Anne murmured as she laid the sleeping baby in her crib. "I'll always make sure you know I'm glad you were born."

A short time later, the doorbell rang, and the postman handed Anne a bulky package. Her heart leaped at the return address. She had never received anything from her mother's address. Her throat squeezed and tears threatened. If she had cried for her mama long ago, she didn't remember it anymore. All she ever felt was an empty place, one of not quite belonging in spite of all the love her aunt and uncle gave her.

Slowly she snipped the tape and pulled the paper away to reveal a worn, somewhat faded baby quilt. Pinned to it was a note that read: "This was made for you when you were born, by my mother, your grandmother. I wanted you to have it for your new baby. Mother."

Anne spread the quilt over the nearby table. She fingered the carefully embroidered animals in each corner of the lovely blending of pink fabrics. Tears mingled with laughter as she looked at her grandmother's handiwork. Someone had rejoiced she was born after all. Her grandmother cared enough to spend hours cutting, piecing, and sewing little pieces of fabric into a pretty design to celebrate her birth. She could picture a gray-headed lady sitting in a rocker stitching love into the fabric. Anne hugged the quilt to herself and danced around the room, singing her own made-up little tune. "Someone was glad I was born. Someone was glad."

Smiling, she tiptoed into the baby's room and gently laid the quilt over the sleeping form. Her daughter stretched a minute and then settled back to sleep. "I'm glad you are here, little one. When I wrap you in this quilt, I'll remember someone cared about me."

No one is unwanted by God. Even before our birth, He cared about us. His love for His people is constant and never fails. He has wrapped us in His love even when we don't feel it. "But the plans of the LORD stand firm forever, the purposes of his heart through all generations" (Psalm 33:11 NIV).

from *The Quilt of Life*
by MARY TATEM

The Sure Afterward

Now no chastening for the present seemeth to be joyous,
but grievous: nevertheless afterward it yieldeth
the peaceable fruit of righteousness unto them
which are exercised thereby.

HEBREWS 12:11

There are some promises which we are apt to reserve for great occasions, and thus lose the continual comfort of them. Perhaps we read this one with a sigh, and say: "How beautiful this is for those whom the Lord is really chastening! I almost think I should not mind that, if such a promise might then be mine. But the things that try me are only little things that turn up every day to trouble and depress me." Well, now, does the Lord specify what degree of trouble, or what kind of trouble, is great enough to make up a claim to the promise? And if He does not, why should you? He only defines it as "not joyous, but grievous." Perhaps there have been a dozen different things today which were "not joyous, but grievous" to you. And though you feel ashamed of feeling them so much, and hardly like to own to their having been so trying, and would not think of signifying them as "chastening," yet, if they come under the Lord's definition, He not only knows all about them, but they were, every one of them, chastenings from His hand; neither to be despised and called "just nothing" when all the while they did "grieve" you; nor to be wearied of; because they are working out blessing to you and glory to Him. Every one of them has been an unrecognized token of His love and interest in you; for "whom the Lord loveth he chasteneth" (Hebrews 12:6).

by FRANCES RIDLEY HAVERGAL

WHAT CONSTITUTES DYNAMIC FAITH?

You believe that God is one.
You do well; the demons also believe, and shudder.
But are you willing to recognize, you foolish fellow,
that faith without works is useless?
Was not Abraham our father justified by works,
when he offered up Isaac his son on the altar?
You see that faith was working with his works,
and as a result of the works, faith was perfected;
and the Scripture was fulfilled which says,
"And Abraham believed God,
and it was reckoned to him as righteousness,"
and he was called the friend of God.
JAMES 2:19–23 NASB

Abraham's faith was evident by his actions. The very foundation of Abraham's faith was the Word of God. And no matter what God required of him, Abraham obeyed God. Therefore, all of his actions were born out of the call God had on his life.

"Faith comes from hearing, and hearing by the word of Christ" (Romans 10:17 NASB). This kind of dynamic faith involves the whole person. If someone professes his or her belief in God and yet does not take the Word to others, and does not attend a weekly Bible study, and can't be bothered to help those in obvious need, it makes one wonder whether that faith is real. For there has to be some outward manifestation of the change that takes place inwardly.

from *Daily Wisdom for Women*
by CAROL FITZPATRICK

CONFLICTS CHANGED TO BLESSINGS

*In all these things we are more than conquerors
through him who loved us.*
ROMANS 8:37 NIV

How can we be "more than conquerors"? We can get out of the conflict a spiritual discipline that will greatly strengthen our faith and establish our spiritual character. Temptation is necessary to settle and confirm us in the spiritual life. It is like the fire which burns in the colors of mineral painting, or like winds that cause the mighty cedars of the mountain to strike more deeply into the soil. Our spiritual conflicts are among our choicest blessings, and our great adversary is used to train us for his ultimate defeat. The ancient Phrygians had a legend that every time they conquered an enemy the victor absorbed the physical strength of his victim and added so much more to his own strength and valor. It is possible thus not only to defeat our enemy, but to capture him and make him fight in our ranks. Just as the wise sailor can use a head wind to carry him forward by tacking and taking advantage of its impelling force, so it is possible for us in our spiritual life through the victorious grace of God to turn to account the things that seem most unfriendly and unfavorable, and to be able to say continually, "The things that were against me have happened to the furtherance of the gospel."

LIFE MORE ABUNDANTLY

from *Streams in the Desert*
by MRS. CHARLES E. COWMAN

FOR THY LOVE IS BETTER THAN WINE

For thy love is better than wine.
SONG OF SOLOMON 1:2

In this place, the word "love" means the continual proofs and tokens of His love, which are said to be better than wine. Wine is a figure of prosperity and of all good and desirable things. The wine from the grape exhilarates and gives strength, but it only strengthens for a time; while the love of Christ is better than all earthly good, and gives divine strength that abides. It is not only the love that He had to usward when He came and died for us; not only the love that He has for those whom He has redeemed; but that enjoyment of His love, which each of those may have who have felt His kiss of reconciliation.

It is entering into deep communion with Him; it is lying at His feet during those moments that are spent alone with Him; it is the consciousness of being well-pleasing to Him and having His love upon us; it is the holy familiarity with which we pour out our own love at His feet, and tell Him all things concerning ourselves. It is at such times that our enraptured souls cry: "Thy love is better than wine!"

No earthly good can allure the one who has pressed close to the side of her Beloved, and has tasted and found that the Lord is good. All the joy and delight, all the pleasures a thousand worlds could offer, are as dust in the balance when weighed against one hour of this mutual exchange of love and communion with the Lord.

by CORA HARRIS MACILRAVY

In the Garden

*When the woman saw that the tree was good for food, and that
it was a delight to the eyes, and that the tree was desirable to
make one wise, she took from its fruit and ate;
and she gave also to her husband with her, and he ate.*

GENESIS 3:6 NASB

On a day she'd never forget, Eve stood beside the "tree of
the knowledge of good and evil" and began listening to
the seductive voice of the crafty serpent. How could she know
that this voice desired to entice her and Adam away from God
and the security of the Garden of Eden? She naïvely chose to
ignore the truth of God's Word and obey that new voice.

And Adam, who loved her, listened to her voice. He then
accepted her invitation to join her in partaking of the fruit of
the tree. As a result, cloaked with garment skins of animals
sacrificed to cover their sin, Adam and Eve were forced out
of this physical garden paradise. Yet the echo of God's loving
promise lingered in their ears. . .a Redeemer would come.

Two thousand years later, Jesus returned to another garden,
choosing it as His place of prayer. Kneeling there, He would
accomplish for men and women this task of abiding in the
Father and obeying His commands. And on the cross the sacrifice of His life provided forgiveness, once again allowing access
to God's presence. . .now within a spiritual garden of prayer.

∞

*Lord, I know I have walked away from You at some point of sin.
That's why You sent Jesus to be my Savior. Forgive me, and enable
me with Your strength to run from sin and toward prayer.*

from *Daily Wisdom for Women*
by CAROL FITZPATRICK

Forgiveness Every Day

*Nevertheless my lovingkindness
will I not utterly take from him,
nor suffer my faithfulness to fail.*
PSALM 89:33

A my tried everything she could to get the little boy to learn to tie his shoes. She had sat with him for hours. There was nothing she could do to make him understand. Finally, she lost all patience and walked off, mad. His shoe-tying education would have to come from someone else with a lot more patience and endurance!

We may give up on each other, but it is comforting to know that God never gives up on us. His offer of forgiveness is open to us today and every day to come. Even though we reject the offer or do things that are frustrating and displeasing to Him, He never gives up. He asks us daily to follow Him until the day we finally do. Thank goodness His patience is without bounds.

∞

Though I push the patience of others to the limits, I am glad to know that I have not pushed Yours, Lord. Continue to forgive me, Lord. I am weak and foolish, and only Your great love keeps me going. Amen.

from *Wisdom from the Psalms*

IF YOU WANT JOY

Thou wilt shew me the path of life:
in thy presence is fulness of joy;
at thy right hand there are pleasures for evermore.
PSALM 16:11

In thy presence is fulness of joy," and fullness of joy is nowhere else. Just as the simple presence of the mother makes the child's joy, so does the simple fact of God's presence with us make our joy. The mother may not make a single promise to the child, nor explain any of her plans or purposes, but she is, and that is enough for the child. The child rejoices in the mother; not in her promises, but in herself. And to the child, there is behind all that changes and can change, the one unchangeable joy of Mother's existence. While the mother lives, the child will be cared for; and the child knows this, instinctively, if not intelligently, and rejoices in knowing it. And to the children of God as well, there is behind all that changes and can change, the one unchangeable joy that God is. And while He is, His children will be cared for, and they ought to know it and rejoice in it, as instinctively and far more intelligently than the child of human parents. For what else can God do, being what He is? Neglect, indifference, forgetfulness, ignorance, are all impossible to Him. He knows everything, He cares about everything, He can manage everything, and He loves us! Surely this is enough for a "fulness of joy" beyond the power of words to express; no matter what else may be missed besides.

by HANNAH WHITALL SMITH

Applying God's Grace to Our Sin

Now if I do that I would not,
it is no more I that do it,
but sin that dwelleth in me.

ROMANS 7:20

Today I feel discouraged and disappointed. I certainly thought that if God really loved me and I really loved Him, I should find myself growing better day by day. But I am not improved in the least. Most of the time I spend on my knees I am either stupid, feeling nothing at all, or else my head is full of what I was doing before I began to pray or what I am going to do as soon as I get through. I do not believe anybody else in the world is like me in this respect. Then when I feel differently and can make a nice, glib prayer, with floods of tears running down my cheeks, I get all puffed up and think how pleased God must be to see me so fervent in spirit. I go downstairs in this frame and begin to complain to our maid, Susan, for misplacing my music, till all of a sudden I catch myself doing it and stop short, crestfallen and confounded. I have so many such experiences that I feel like a baby just learning to walk, who is so afraid of falling that it has half a mind to sit down once and for all.

from *Stepping Heavenward*
by ELIZABETH PRENTISS

A DAILY DOSE

I have hidden your word in my heart
that I might not sin against you.
PSALM 119:11 NIV

I wish someone would invent a "fruit-of-the-Spirit" pill. That way, each morning I could just pop one in, and all day long I would bubble over with love, joy, faith, patience, and so on. I know it would sell. The bottle label could say, "One a day keeps the grouchies away!" My family would be the first to stock up!

Some days I just seem to wake up with my claws extended. I proceed to snap, criticize, and generally spread gloom and frustration. And of course I'm very adept at blaming my sour mood on something or someone else. The culprit is either hormones, lack of sleep, my husband, my children, the price of tea in China, or all of the above.

By the end of the day, I'm usually so miserable that tears come easily and I'm forced to withdraw for a few moments of self-examination. And almost without fail I discover that the root of the problem is that I've become unplugged—unplugged from the only power source that can conquer daily life as we know it. Maybe I find that I've neglected my quiet time with the Master. Whatever the specifics, the bottom line is that I should be taking my "fruit-of-the-Spirit" pill—which means quality time spent in prayer and Bible study, seeking God's will.

from *Time Out*
by LEIGH ANN THOMAS

HIS MAGNIFICENT CREATION

But thou, O LORD, art a shield for me;
my glory, and the lifter up of mine head.
PSALM 3:3

I was walking along one day, deeply troubled and feeling quite alone. Pressures and problems seemed too much to bear, and I found nothing to make me feel hopeful. My deep thought was broken by a flutter of wings and a flash of color. A butterfly flitted in front of my face, then alighted on my shoulder. The grace and beauty of the small creature broke through my depression and caused me to smile. The great weight I was feeling in my heart lifted, and I began chastising myself for having been so foolish. In a world where such glory exists, why do we continually allow worldly concerns to occupy so much of our attentions? Let God be our glory, and indeed, when we find ourselves most down, He will lift our heads up and show us all the wonders of His magnificent creation.

∞

Lord, protect me from those things that turn my attention from You. Clear the eyes of my heart so they can focus on the splendor of Your creation. Thank You for the blessings of this day. Amen.

from *Wisdom from the Psalms*

OUR THOUGHTS

Whatsoever things are true, whatsoever things are honest,
whatsoever things are just, whatsoever things are pure,
whatsoever things are lovely,
whatsoever things are of good report;
if there be any virtue, and if there be any praise,
think on these things.
PHILIPPIANS 4:8

The things we think on are the things that feed our souls. If we think on pure and lovely things, we shall grow pure and lovely like them; and the converse is equally true. Very few people at all realize this, and consequently there is a great deal of carelessness, even with careful people, in regard to their thoughts. They guard their words and actions with the utmost care, but their thoughts, which, after all, are the very spring and root of everything in character and life, they neglect entirely. So long as it is not put into spoken words, it seems of no consequence at all what goes on within the mind. No one hears or knows, and therefore they imagine that the vagrant thoughts that come and go as they list, do no harm. Such persons are very careless as to the food offered to their thoughts, and accept haphazardly, without discrimination, anything that comes.

Every thought we think, in every hour we live, must be, not necessarily about Christ, but it must be the thought Christ would think were He placed in our circumstances and subject to our conditions. This is what it means really to feed on Him and be nourished by the true Bread of Life that cometh down from heaven.

by HANNAH WHITALL SMITH

LIGHTHOUSES

The people which sat in darkness saw great light.
MATTHEW 4:16

When we think of lighthouses, most of us think of stormy New England coasts or the treacherous beaches of North Carolina's Outer Banks. In fact, though, some of the most elaborate lighthouses were built thousands of years ago in Asia.

The Pharos of Alexandria, one of the Seven Wonders of the World, is said to have been the world's first lighthouse. It was constructed in Alexandria, Egypt, during the third century before Christ, commissioned by Ptolemy, the Macedonian ruler of Egypt. Made from three square sections, it reached a total height of 450 feet and measured 360 feet on each side.

Imagine what this immense lighthouse must have looked like blazing out against the absolute darkness of nights that were unlit by any electricity. For more than fifteen hundred years, it guided mariners to safety, its light visible from a distance of a hundred miles.

Like those long-ago Egyptians, sometimes we seem to live in a world of total darkness. But we, too, have a great and powerful Lighthouse that illumines our nights. No matter how far we travel from Him, His light is still visible, always ready to guide us back to safety.

from *A Beacon of Hope*
by ELLYN SANNA

GOD'S MESSAGE TO THE CHURCHES

"But I have this against you,
that you have left your first love."
REVELATION 2:4 NASB

One of my favorite questions to ask couples over dinner is "How did you meet?" Each story invariably presents a set of impossible circumstances that had to be orchestrated in order to bring this man and woman together. As these details are relayed, a glow begins to come back into the eyes of those remembering. There is nothing to compare with that "first bloom of love."

This is the kind of love which God desires from us. That on-fire, totally consuming, single focus of our attention. His call to the church at Ephesus then was that they remember their first love—and rekindle their purpose to seek Him first.

His message, however, to the church at Smyrna was very different: "I know your tribulation and your poverty (but you are rich). . . Do not fear what you are about to suffer. . . . Be faithful until death, and I will give you the crown of life" (Revelation 2:9–10 NASB).

Throughout history, God's church has suffered persecution. But here is a message of hope to all for whom cruelty is a constant companion: "Remain faithful; God's reward is at hand."

from *Daily Wisdom for Women*
by CAROL FITZPATRICK

OUR ALLY

I will not be afraid of ten thousands of people,
that have set themselves against me round about.
PSALM 3:6

All of the customers had been so hateful and belligerent. Nancy thought that if one more unpleasant person assaulted her, she would scream. To make matters worse, the store owners were being unreasonable and hard to get along with. She didn't know how much more she could take. She rested her chin on her chest and heaved a heavy sigh. Then, the cross she wore around her neck caught her eye, and she felt strangely calm. The frustrations of the day melted away as the peace of Christ settled upon her heart.

In the daily battles we find ourselves engaged in, it is vital that we remember we have an ally who is greater than anyone who might oppose us or wish to make us unhappy. Jesus Christ became victor over everything this world could throw at Him; even death itself. If we will give Him control of our hearts, He will be true to us and grant us victory in the struggles we face.

∞

Father, You have made me a conqueror through Your Son, Jesus Christ. Help me to live as a victor and not as one defeated. Lift me up to be a sign to the world that in Christ we need never be afraid. Amen.

from *Wisdom from the Psalms*

AGAINST THE CURRENT

So likewise,
whosoever he be of you that forsaketh not all that he hath,
he cannot be my disciple.

LUKE 14:33

You must remember that our God has all knowledge and all wisdom, and that therefore it is very possible He may guide you into paths wherein He knows great blessings are awaiting you, but which, to the shortsighted human eyes around you, seem sure to result in confusion and loss. You must recognize the fact that God's thoughts are not as man's thoughts, nor His ways as man's ways; and that He alone, who knows the end of things from the beginning, can judge what the results of any course of action may be. You must, therefore, realize that His very love for you may perhaps lead you to run counter to the loving wishes of even your dearest friends. You must learn, from Luke 14:26–33, and similar passages, that in order to be a disciple and follower of your Lord, you may perhaps be called upon to forsake inwardly all that you have, even father or mother, or brother or sister, or husband or wife, or it may be your own life also. Unless the possibility of this is clearly recognized, you will be very likely to get into difficulty, because it often happens that the child of God who enters upon this life of obedience is sooner or later led into paths which meet with the disapproval of those he best loves; and unless he is prepared for this, and can trust the Lord through it all, he will scarcely know what to do.

from *The Christian's Secret of a Happy Life*
by HANNAH WHITALL SMITH

God's Precious Promises

His divine power has granted to us everything pertaining
to life and godliness, through the true knowledge
of Him who called us by His own glory and excellence.
For by these He has granted to us
His precious and magnificent promises,
in order that by them you might become partakers
of the divine nature, having escaped the corruption
that is in the world by lust.
2 Peter 1:3–4 NASB

From the moment a baby is conceived, it has everything it needs to grow into a complete human being, everything except time. For time acts as a refiner. Our spiritual growth is the same. From the moment we accept Christ, He infuses His Spirit within us, giving us right standing with the Father and making us children of God. "He made Him who knew no sin to be sin on our behalf, that we might become the righteousness of God in Him" (2 Corinthians 5:21 NASB). As we walk in step with Him, learning His ways, we will eventually reflect these changes in our character.

Peter reminds us that Jesus Christ is the Savior. "Therefore, brethren, be all the more diligent to make certain about His calling and choosing you; for as long as you practice these things, you will never stumble; for in this way the entrance into the eternal kingdom of our Lord and Savior Jesus Christ will be abundantly supplied to you" (2 Peter 1:10–11 NASB).

from *Daily Wisdom for Women*
by Carol Fitzpatrick

A Guardian Angel

For he shall give his angels charge over thee,
to keep thee in all thy ways.
PSALM 91:11

Louise had an angel. She felt the presence of her guardian angel wherever she was. She didn't even tell most people about her angel, because they looked at her like she was crazy when she did. She wasn't. God had sent her an angel to keep her company and to remind her that she was loved. There was nothing crazy about that. Sometimes, in the still of the night, she thought she could hear angel songs, and they comforted her. She loved her angel, and she thanked God for it daily.

Who's to say where God's angels are? Perhaps we each have an angel who watches us and guides us. God, in His love for us, has set the angels over us. They are His ambassadors of goodwill in this world. Though angels have been shoved aside to the category of myth by many, we know that there is another realm where everything doesn't always make sense to us. Rest secure. The angels are watching.

∞

Help me to believe in the angels that You send, Lord. I need watching over. I need You to be with me. I thank You for guiding me in all my ways. Amen.

from *Wisdom from the Psalms*

Let My Roots Sink Deep

The LORD is my shepherd; I shall not want.
He maketh me to lie down in green pastures:
he leadeth me beside the still waters.

PSALM 23:1–2

Lord, I sit alone by a quiet stream. My thoughts turn to Psalm 23. The waters gently ripple by. Trees gracefully bow their branches and teasingly rustle their leaves in the pure, fresh breeze. A bird lilts a beckoning call to its mate. A distant falcon pierces the air with its echoing screech.

Peace. Thank You, Lord. But what about when I must return to the hustle and bustle? How can I be prepared?

I look at the trees; their roots sink deep by the stream. In the same way, let my roots sink deep into You. Let me feed on Your Word. As we commune in prayer, let me drink from the living water of Your spirit. Let me jump in and be bathed by Your cleansing power. I will rely on You rather than things that are shallow and temporary. I can't depend on my own abilities and strength, but I'm confident in Your care and direction.

I will take special notice of the good things when they come. I will fix my mind on what is pure and lovely and upright.

When the heat and winds of life's storms come, I will not fear; I know You are near. I will not worry but keep on producing a life that is a blessing for You and others.

Let me take time often to come drink from Your quiet stream. I thank You for it.

from *When I'm on My Knees*
by ANITA CORRINE DONIHUE

Turn Your Ear to Wisdom

For the LORD gives wisdom;
from His mouth come knowledge and understanding.
He stores up sound wisdom for the upright;
He is a shield to those who walk in integrity,
guarding the paths of justice,
and He preserves the way of His godly ones.
PROVERBS 2:6–8 NASB

Every family has at least one relative who cannot get his act together. (Meanwhile the rest of us scratch our heads and wonder how he can miss the obvious, every single time.) It's as though these people have to fall in every pothole in the street because it never occurs to them to go down a different road.

Are you smiling yet? Is someone in particular coming clearly into focus? Now, hold that thought.

God's Word says wisdom is truly a gift since it comes from the mouth of God, from the very words He speaks. And all God's words have been written down for us, through the inspiration of the Holy Spirit. Therefore, those who refuse to accept God's guidance, who refuse to ask for His wisdom—those hapless relatives, perhaps—will never see the light of reality.

Know that if you hold fast to the precepts contained in the Bible, you will walk in integrity. Instead of gravitating toward potholes, your feet will be planted on the straight and narrow road.

Lord, I can't change my relatives, but I can change myself. So, if my head is the one peeking out of the pothole, please pull me out!

from *Daily Wisdom for Women*
by CAROL FITZPATRICK

As Peaceful As a Flower

Whosoever shall not receive the kingdom of God
as a little child shall in no wise enter therein.
LUKE 18:17

We complicate our lives when we borrow trouble from the future. We waste our energy worrying about what might happen tomorrow; we become frantic and pressured looking at the many responsibilities on our to-do list for the next week; we lie awake obsessing over our plans for the upcoming month.

And meanwhile we miss the precious gift of peace that God has given us right here, right now, in this tiny present moment that touches eternity. Be like the wildflowers, Jesus tells us in the Gospels, simply soaking up today's sunshine: "Take therefore no thought for the morrow: for the morrow shall take thought for the things of itself" (Matthew 6:34).

Children live the same way, delighting in the here and now, untroubled by the future. When we can find that same wholehearted simplicity, we too will know the peace of God's kingdom.

from *Keep It Simple*
by ELLYN SANNA

Joining Our Will with God's

*Teach me to do thy will; for thou art my God: thy spirit is good;
lead me into the land of uprightness.*
PSALM 143:10

I cannot make myself holy; only Christ can do that. But I can choose to exercise my will for God. Just as a married couple commits themselves to each other, I commit myself to Christ. This is an active decision, one that affects the way I live my entire life. Like marriage, however, it is not a decision that can be made once and then be done with it; instead, I must choose to commit myself to God's will daily.

from *Stepping Heavenward*
by ELIZABETH PRENTISS

Meek and Lowly

Take my yoke upon you, and learn of me;
for I am meek and lowly in heart:
and ye shall find rest unto your souls.
MATTHEW 11:29

What can be more delicious to a delicate self-love than to hear itself applauded for having none! The truly meek and lowly heart does not want to talk about its ME at all, either for good or evil. It wants to forget its very existence. As Fenelon writes, it says to this ME, "I do not know you, and am not interested in you. You are a stranger to me, and I do not care what happens to you nor how you are treated." If people slight you or treat you with contempt or neglect, the meek and lowly heart accepts all as its rightful portion. True humility makes us love to be treated, both by God and man, as we feel our imperfections really deserve; and, instead of resenting such treatment, we welcome it and are thankful for it. I remember being greatly struck by a saying of Madame Guyon's, that she had learned to give thanks for every mortification that befell her, because she had found mortifications so helpful in putting self to death. It is undoubtedly true, as another old saint says, that there is no way attaining the grace of humility but by the way of humiliations. Humiliations are the medicine that the Great Physician generally administers to cure the spiritual dropsy caused by feeding the soul on continual thoughts of ME.

by HANNAH WHITALL SMITH

SORROW'S SCARS

Now after the death of Moses
the servant of the LORD it came to pass,
that the LORD spake unto Joshua the son of Nun,
Moses' minister, saying, Moses my servant is dead;
now therefore arise, go over this Jordan,
thou, and all this people.
JOSHUA 1:1–2

Sorrow came to you yesterday, and emptied your home. Your first impulse is to give up and sit down in despair amid the wrecks of your hopes. But you dare not do it. You are in the line of battle and the crisis is at hand. . . .

Weeping inconsolably beside a grave can never give back love's banished treasure, nor can any blessing come out of such sadness. Yet there is a humanizing and fertilizing influence in sorrow which has been rightly accepted and cheerfully borne. Indeed, they are poor who have never suffered and have none of sorrow's marks upon them. The joy set before us should shine upon our grief as the sun shines through the clouds, glorifying them. God has so ordered, that in pressing on in duty we shall find the truest, richest comfort for ourselves. Sitting down to brood over our sorrows, the darkness deepens about us and creeps into our heart, and our strength changes to weakness. But, if we turn away from the gloom, and take up the tasks and duties to which God calls us, the light will come again, and we shall grow stronger.

J. R. MILLER

from *Streams in the Desert*
by MRS. CHARLES E. COWMAN

COMPELLED TO PRAY

*Do not be anxious about anything, but in everything, by prayer
and petition, with thanksgiving, present your requests to God.*
PHILIPPIANS 4:6 NIV

I don't go very long without a diet soft drink in my hand.
When I feel the need for something to drink, nothing gets
in my way until my thirst is quenched.

In the same way, sometimes my soul feels so dry that I
long to drink in the soothing, soul-quenching grace of the
Holy Spirit. The need becomes so strong that I drop what
I'm doing and slip away to a private place—the bedroom, the
bathroom, or the back porch.

When I go to my Father, I am never disappointed. He
reveals to me my innermost self. He shows me the burdens
that I thought I had laid at His feet, but which I later took
back upon myself. He reminds me of the needs of others,
that perhaps I had promised to pray for but didn't. He listens
as I confess what He already knew. He restores my soul.

One of my favorite verses is, "For it is God who works in
you to will and to act according to his good purpose" (Philippians 2:13 NIV). When I have a longing to pray, it's not
because of anything I've done. . .but because my Creator is
moving in me. What an awesome thought! It never ceases to
amaze me that God actually takes the time to notice
insignificant me and to draw me closer to Him. What's even
more amazing is that to God I'm not insignificant at all. In
fact, even when the whole world may be against me, my
Lord thinks I'm pretty special. Wow, what a Savior!

from *Time Out*
by LEIGH ANN THOMAS

The Early Hours

My voice shalt thou hear in the morning, O LORD;
in the morning will I direct my prayer unto thee,
and will look up.

PSALM 5:3

The sun had just begun to climb into the sky, and the dew shone brightly on the field below. Though not ordinarily a morning person, Ann always loved those special times when she rose in time to see the sunrise. *On mornings like this, who could doubt that there is a God?* Ann's heart filled with a joy beyond words, and nothing could remove that joy during the day. Taking a Bible, she went to a clearing to sit and to read and to pray.

God gives us special times in order that we might find joy and that we might find Him. He has created a glorious world, and He has freely given it to us. The early quiet of the day is a beautiful time to encounter the Lord. Give Him your early hours, and He will give you all the blessings you can hold.

∞

I raise my voice to You in the morning, Lord. Help me to appreciate Your new day, and use it to the fullest. Open my eyes to the splendor of all Your creation. Amen.

from *Wisdom from the Psalms*

THE GIFT OF LIFE

Every good gift and every perfect gift is from above,
and cometh down from the Father of lights.
JAMES 1:17

I would say, first of all, that this blessed life must not be looked upon in any sense as an attainment, but as an obtainment. We cannot earn it, we cannot climb up to it, we cannot win it; we can do nothing but ask for it and receive it. It is the gift of God in Christ Jesus. And where a thing is a gift, the only course left for the receiver is to take it and thank the giver. We never say of a gift, "See to what I have attained," and boast of our skill and wisdom in having attained it; but we say, "See what has been given me," and boast of the love and wealth and generosity of the giver. And everything in our salvation is a gift. From beginning to end, God is the giver and we are the receivers; and it is not to those who do great things, but to those who "receive abundance of grace and of the gift of righteousness," that the richest promises are made.

from *The Christian's Secret of a Happy Life*
by HANNAH WHITALL SMITH

OUR ADVOCATE AND DEFENDER

"Everyone therefore who shall confess Me before men,
I will also confess him before My Father who is in heaven.
But whoever shall deny Me before men,
I will also deny him before My Father who is in heaven."
MATTHEW 10:32–33 NASB

My sisters and I attended private schools for most of our lives but that did not render us immune to rowdies or bullies. And since we walked a few miles to school each day, we were at times easy prey.

Busy with friends her own age, my older sister didn't usually accompany my younger sister and me on our morning trek.

However, when we returned home one day relating that two big kids from the nearby public school had threatened to beat us up the next day, she rallied to the cause. As she instructed, we traversed our normal route while she lagged watchfully a short distance behind.

Suddenly the two boys jumped out of the bushes ahead. And just like a superwoman, our sister pounced on them, easily overpowering both and giving them bloody noses in the process. I'll never forget that scene as long as I live. It felt so incredible to have an invincible defender!

If we know Jesus Christ and have responded to His invitation to receive Him as Savior, Jesus remains forever our advocate before the Father, saying with love, "She's mine." Know that you are so precious to Jesus that He gave His life for you. Doesn't it feel incredible to have Jesus as your defender?

from *Daily Wisdom for Women*
by CAROL FITZPATRICK

Amazing Grace

I have blotted out, as a thick cloud, thy transgressions, and,
as a cloud, thy sins: return unto me; for I have redeemed thee.

Isaiah 44:22

He will turn again,
he will have compassion upon us;
he will subdue our iniquities;
and thou wilt cast all their sins
into the depths of the sea.

Micah 7:19

If my shut eyes should dare their lids to part,
I know how they must quail beneath the blaze
Of Thy love's greatness. No; I dare not raise
One prayer, to look aloft, lest it should gaze
On such forgiveness as would break my heart.

H. S. Sutton

O Lord God, gracious and merciful, give us, I entreat Thee, a hum-
ble trust in Thy mercy, and suffer not our heart to fail us. Though
our sins be seven, though our sins be seventy times seven, though our
sins be more in number than the hairs of our head, yet give us grace
in loving penitence to cast ourselves down into the depth of Thy
compassion. Let us fall into the hand of the Lord. Amen.

Christina G. Rossetti

compiled by Mary W. Tileston

PUTTING ON THE ARMOR

Put on the whole armour of God,
that ye may be able to stand against the wiles of the devil.
EPHESIANS 6:11

Eileen loved to roller-blade. She kept up with the best of them. For Christmas and birthdays she had received all the proper gear from her parents in order to blade safely: a helmet and shoulder, elbow, wrist, knee, and shin guards. Her family made sure that she had all the necessities. They knew what could happen.

One nice afternoon Eileen had a half hour free. In a hurry, she grabbed all her gear except the wrist guards that had fallen in the corner.

It wasn't long until Eileen hit a curb wrong and went flying. Sure enough, she broke her wrist.

It's the same way with our armor from God. We can't live victorious lives unless we put on all His armor. It won't work with everything but faith. Neither will we see victory in Jesus without knowing or telling the truth—or neglecting to obey God with a righteous life. And we certainly will have no protection if we are not saved in Jesus Christ. What about peace? How many times have you hung your head in sadness over someone who says he loves the Lord but is gossiping and stirring up trouble instead of carrying a message of peace?

The devil knows our weakest spots. If we don't daily clothe ourselves completely in God's spiritual armor when we hit the rough bumps—sure enough—we come crashing down. That weak spot is bound to be injured.

So as you dress for your day and pray, remember to put on every single piece of God's armor. Then listen to Him.

from *When I'm Praising God*
by ANITA CORRINE DONIHUE

Be Made Whole

Have mercy upon me, O LORD;
for I am weak; O LORD, heal me;
for my bones are vexed.

PSALM 6:2

The closer we get to God, the more glaring are our faults. The brighter the light of perfection that we subject ourselves to, the more flaws are revealed. The better we understand the awesome magnificence of God, the more we expose our own imperfection. As the great men and women of the Bible came to realize, the stronger we become in the faith, the more wretched we sometimes feel.

This, however, is no cause for despair. Our Lord wants nothing more than for us to come to depend on Him. We can only truly become dependent as we acknowledge our inadequacies. As the apostle Paul found out, true strength comes from admitting our weakness, and total healing comes by realizing that without God we are sickly and terminally diseased by sin. Cry out for the mercy of God and He will strengthen you; ask for His healing and you will be made whole.

∞

Dear Lord, I try to be perfect and find that I am hopelessly deficient. Nothing I can do will bring me the perfection You intend for me. Fill me with Your Spirit and do for me all that I cannot do for myself. Amen.

from *Wisdom from the Psalms*

No Fear

If ye had known me, ye should have known my Father also:
and from henceforth ye know him,
and have seen him.

JOHN 14:7

A friend of mine told me that her childhood was passed in a perfect terror of God. Her idea of Him was that He was a cruel giant with an awful "Eye" which could see everything, no matter how it might be hidden, and that He was always spying upon her, and watching for chances to punish her, and to snatch away all her joys.

With a child's strange reticence, she never told anyone of her terror; but one night Mother, coming into the room unexpectedly, heard the poor little despairing cry, and, with a sudden comprehension of what it meant, sat down beside the bed, and, taking the cold little hand in hers, told her God was not a dreadful tyrant to be afraid of, but was just like Jesus; and that she knew how good and kind Jesus was, and how He loved little children, and took them in His arms and blessed them. My friend said she had always loved the stories about Jesus, and when she heard that God was like Him, it was a perfect revelation to her, and took away her fear of God forever. She went about all that day saying to herself over and over, "Oh, I am so glad I have found out that God is like Jesus, for Jesus is so nice. Now I need never be afraid of God anymore."

The little child had got a sight of God "in the face of Jesus Christ," and it brought rest to her soul.

by HANNAH WHITALL SMITH

A Bountiful Blending

*And we know that all things work together
for good to them that love God.*
ROMANS 8:28

How wide is this assertion of the apostle Paul! He does not say, "We know that some things," or "most things," but "all things." From the minutest to the most momentous; from the humblest event in daily providence to the great crisis-hours in grace.

And all things "work"—they are working; not all things have worked, or shall work; but it is a present operation.

At this very moment, when some voice may be saying, "Thy judgments are a great deep," the angels above, who are watching the development of the great plan, are with folded wings exclaiming, "The LORD is righteous in all his ways, and holy in all his works" (Psalm 145:17).

And then all things "work together." It is a beautiful blending. Many different colors, in themselves raw and unsightly, are required in order to weave the harmonious pattern.

Many separate wheels and joints are required to make the piece of machinery. Take a thread separately, or a note separately, or a wheel or a tooth of a wheel separately, and there may be neither use nor beauty discernible.

But complete the web, combine the notes, put together the separate parts of steel and iron, and you see how perfect and symmetrical is the result. Here is the lesson for faith: "What I do thou knowest not now, but thou shalt know hereafter" (Macduff).

from *Streams in the Desert*
by MRS. CHARLES E. COWMAN

WHO, ME?

Being confident of this, that he who began a good work in you will carry it on to completion until the day of Christ Jesus.
PHILIPPIANS 1:6 NIV

The hardest thing for me to accept in my Christian walk is that Almighty God, Creator of heaven and earth, actually has a plan and a life's work prepared for me. It's so much easier to believe and rejoice in how He's working in other lives. You know, other more "qualified" people. I have no problem believing in the life, death, and resurrection of Jesus Christ. I believe He loved this world enough to pay the ultimate price for our sin by laying down His life. But for some reason, I sometimes have trouble believing that He wants to use me. I feel inadequate so much of the time. I mean, I've been known to snap at my children and be angry with my husband. My house is a mess, I bite my nails, and sometimes I speak before I think. How can God use me when I feel so incompetent?

When feelings of inadequacy threaten to overwhelm me, I cling to the Scriptures. I read about those men and women in Bible times whom God used to carry out His will. I think about Moses, whom used his speech defect as an excuse to God. I think of David, who was only a shepherd boy. And then there was Sarah, who laughed when God's messengers said she was to bear a child, and Rebekah, who encouraged her own son to be deceitful to his father. In spite of their human frailties, God used these men and women and many others to accomplish His purposes.

So let us remind ourselves often: God can use me; God can use you. All He requires is a willing heart, totally committed to Him.

from *Time Out*
by LEIGH ANN THOMAS

How Can We Praise in Faith-Believing?

For we walk by faith, not by sight.
2 CORINTHIANS 5:7

When the odds seem impossible to overcome, we carefully, painfully seek God's will. But how do we go about actively praising Him in faith-believing? Is it an attitude? Words? Or does it go beyond that?

Faith soars above the mountains of uncertainty and utters a confidence and assurance in our Lord God. He has a precise way of tunneling through, going over or around, and finding the answers. Although we don't know what is around the next bend, we must give Him our unconditional trust.

Putting our faith in action and praising Him for answers to come means plugging up the hill and doing the best we can as we trust Him in the trek. Other times, it is going ahead in faith-believing, knowing without a shadow of doubt what He has for us, even if it's outside our comfort zone! Either way, we must take time to rest our minds and emotions, becoming refreshed in His strengthening Holy Spirit.

The most difficult part for me in putting faith into action and praising Him for answers to come is when I must completely turn all over to God and take my hands off. But what often comes is a time when I hear God say, "Hands off and let Me."

It is at this point where I learn to actively praise Him for helping, actively rest in His will and timing, actively trust Him to fight the battles as I learn to sit back and go along for the ride.

from *When I'm Praising God*
by ANITA CORRINE DONIHUE

His Wonderful Works

I will praise thee, O LORD, with my whole heart;
I will shew forth all thy marvellous works.
PSALM 9:1

Audrey loved the little children, and they dearly loved her. She would walk with them through the gardens and fields, showing them all the wonders of nature. She would sit with them for hours and tell them stories. She would read to them from her Bible, then explain what she had read. She would remind the children of all the good things God could do. For the main part of her life, Audrey taught little children the reality of God.

To be truly in love with God is a consuming passion. We can't wait to tell the world of the wonderful truth we know. The Spirit of God enters in, and our lives are never the same again. Praise the Lord with your whole heart, and show forth all His wonderful works.

∽

Each new day brings new wonders to my attention. Thank You, O Lord, for creating such a beautiful world with so many miracles to behold. Amen.

from *Wisdom from the Psalms*

WHAT THINK YE OF CHRIST?

What think ye of Christ?
MATTHEW 22:42

The crucial question for each one of us in our everyday life is just this, "What think ye of Christ?" To some, the question may seem to require a doctrinal answer, and I do not at all say that there is no idea of doctrine involved in it. But to my mind, the doctrinal answer, valuable as it may be, is not the one of most importance for every day. The vital answer is the one that would contain our own personal knowledge of the character of Christ; not what He is doctrinally, but what He is intrinsically, in Himself. For, after all, our salvation does not depend upon the doctrines concerning Christ, but upon the person of Christ Himself, what He is and upon what He does.

"For the which cause I also suffer these things: nevertheless I am not ashamed: for I know whom I have believed, and am persuaded that he is able to keep that which I have committed unto him against that day" (2 Timothy 1:12).

Paul knew Christ; therefore, Paul could trust Him; and if we would trust Him as Paul did, we must know Him as intimately. I am afraid a great many people are so taken up with Christian doctrines and dogmas, and are so convinced that their salvation is secured because their "views" are sound and orthodox, that they have never yet come to a personal acquaintance with Christ Himself.

by HANNAH WHITALL SMITH

ANGELS

Take heed that ye despise not one of these little ones;
for I say unto you,
That in heaven their angels do always
behold the face of my Father which is in heaven.
MATTHEW 18:10

Angels are all around us in the form of gold pins on shoulders, other kinds of jewelry and pictures, and in stores, books, poetry, and even movies.

The Bible tells us real angels are here with us. Some of us have even experienced angels working personally in our lives. The Bible also teaches we are a little lower than the angels, but God has appointed angels and us both to be servants for Him.

We must be careful that our praise does not go to the angels, but only to God who made them. Remember, the Scriptures tell us we are to put nothing or no one before God. This includes angels.

God is the Master of all. Him only are we to worship and serve.

Let's be thankful for angels, but be thankful to God who made them.

from *When I'm Praising God*
by ANITA CORRINE DONIHUE

Where's Home?

Thou wilt shew me the path of life:
in thy presence is fulness of joy;
at thy right hand there are pleasures for evermore.
PSALM 16:11

I liked our house in Virginia better," Kara whined as the Johnsons' car stopped behind the moving van in the driveway of the family's new house.

"You'll have a bigger room all to yourself in this house." Mother kept her voice cheerful.

"I'll share a room with Kara if I can move back to Virginia. Texas doesn't have any trees. Virginia's better," Rachel agreed with her younger sister.

"The Air Force needs Daddy to live in San Antonio for a while. And there are too trees. There's one right in our front yard."

"Not lots of trees like Virginia." Kara stuffed her thumb in her mouth.

"We'll have fun finding out what fun things we can do in our new state." Loraine Johnson's patience was wearing thin.

"It's not fun if I can't play with Tammy." Rachel's pout matched Kara's. "She's not in Texas."

Mother sighed. "I know you miss your friend, but you'll meet some wonderful new ones here. Let's go inside and see if the movers have set up your beds."

"I'll get lost at night trying to find the bathroom," Kara complained as the girls trailed behind their mother up the stairs to find their father.

To Loraine's relief, the furniture in both the girls' rooms was in place. "Here's the box marked sheets and quilts," Loraine said. "Let's make your beds first thing."

The girls grabbed their quilts with glad cries when Mother

pulled them from the carton.

Kara lay down on her bed after her mother spread the quilt over the clean sheets and smiled. "It's fun to be by myself," she said as her sister and mother stepped across the hall to make Rachel's bed.

"It feels like home, now," Rachel said. "I love my doggy quilt."

Loraine Johnson sighed with relief at the difference in her girls' attitudes. They began to explore their new house with enthusiasm instead of complaints.

On future moves, the first item of business for this military family was to set up and make the girls' beds. Somehow the presence of their quilts on a familiar piece of furniture established security for the children and smoothed the way for adjustments.

When we sense God's presence in our lives, we enjoy a secure feeling and adjust to the changes life brings. Since change is one of the guarantees of life, we need to learn to find His presence and become comfortable in it. His presence helps us adjust to the unexpected.

from *The Quilt of Life*
by MARY TATEM

THE ROMANCE OF RELIGIOUS LIFE

For the which cause I also suffer these things:
nevertheless I am not ashamed:
for I know whom I have believed,
and am persuaded that he is able to keep that
which I have committed unto him against that day.
2 TIMOTHY 1:12

My soul had started on its voyage of discovery, and to become acquainted with God was its unalterable and unceasing aim. I was as yet only at the beginning, but what a magnificent beginning it was. God was a reality, and He was my God. He had created me, and He loved me, and all was right between us. All care about my own future destiny had been removed from my shoulders. I could say with Paul, "I know whom I have believed, and am persuaded that he is able to keep that which I have committed unto him against that day." I needed no longer to work for my soul's salvation, but only to work out the salvation that had been bestowed upon me. All the years of my self-introversion and self-examination were ended. Instead of my old fruitless searchings into my feelings and emotions for some tangible evidence of God's favor, the glorious news, declared in the Bible, that He so loved the world as to have sent His only begotten Son to save the world, absorbed every faculty.

It was no longer "How do I feel?" but always "What does God say?" And He said such delightful things, that to find them out became my supreme delight.

by HANNAH WHITALL SMITH

OUR REFUGE

The LORD also will be a refuge for the oppressed,
a refuge in times of trouble.
PSALM 9:9

Ellen lived in a tiny shack on the edge of a small backwater town. She had no modern conveniences; no car, no electricity, no fancy clothing. She just lived a simple life, giving of herself to others, sharing what little she did have with anyone who needed it. Often people tried to help Ellen, but she just smiled and said she didn't want for anything. When asked why she lived as she did, Ellen said, "God has made sure that I've had enough to get by on. I don't need any more than that. He and I have a nice deal. When He needs me, He lets me know and shows me what I can do, and when I need Him, all I have to do is call. I've faced hard times, but the Lord has always given me strength and given me a place to run to."

The Lord is our refuge and our strength. It takes a great deal of wisdom to realize that. Our lives are much more than possessions and positions. Our lives are gifts from God; given to us and to others for His glory. We need not ask what more God can do for us, but what we might do for God. He will surely let us know.

∞

Father, I sometimes need to escape: from the world, from myself, from the things that tie me down. Be my liberation and my sanctuary. Strengthen me for Your service. Amen.

from *Wisdom from the Psalms*

WISDOM COMES FROM GOD

And coming to His home town
He began teaching them in their synagogue,
so that they became astonished, and said,
"Where did this man get this wisdom,
and these miraculous powers?"
MATTHEW 13:54 NASB

The toughest critics you'll ever encounter are family and friends. The reason is simple: They know you best. When vulnerability swings your trapeze with such speed that your grip loosens, they watch as you fall. At that moment, you can stand there gazing at your flattened imprint in the dirt or climb up the ladder and try again.

Yes, some will continue to stare, waiting for you to stumble once again, but there will be new faces in your crowd of onlookers. They believe you can reach your goals and make a difference in our world.

Jesus encountered these same narrow-minded pessimists, those who claimed they knew Him from way back. Ridiculing Him, they said, "Isn't He just a carpenter's son?" Yes, He surely was, but that carpenter was the Master Builder! For Jesus wasn't Joseph's son, but God's Son.

He came from God, full of wisdom. Those who stood with Him during His earthly ministry had true wisdom and understanding from God. They made up His true family of believers. Today, you obtain wisdom through a personal knowledge of Christ and by studying His Word. For only then can God's Spirit fill you with the wisdom you'll need to find and live out your God-given purpose.

from *Daily Wisdom for Women*
by CAROL FITZPATRICK

An Inflexible Will

For it is God who works in you to will
and to act according to his good purpose.
PHILIPPIANS 2:13 NIV

It has been said "that a fixed, inflexible will is a great assistance in a holy life."

You can will to use every means of grace appointed by God.

You can will to spend much time in prayer without regard to your frame at the moment.

You can will to prefer a religion of principle to one of mere feeling; in other words, to obey the will of God when no comfortable glow of emotion accompanies your obedience.

You cannot will to possess the spirit of Christ; that must come as His gift; but you can choose to study His life and imitate it. This will infallibly lead to such self-denying work as visiting the poor, nursing the sick, giving of your time and money to the needy, and the like.

If the thought of such self-denial is repugnant to you, remember that it is enough for the disciple to be as his Lord. And let me assure you that as you penetrate the labyrinth of life in pursuit of Christian duty, you will often be surprised and charmed by meeting your Master Himself amid its windings and turnings and receive His soul-inspiring smile. Or, I should rather say, you will always meet Him, wherever you go.

from *Stepping Heavenward*
by ELIZABETH PRENTISS

THE CROSS IN THE CENTER

He humbled himself, and became obedient unto death,
even the death of the cross.

PHILIPPIANS 2:8

Look at the cross. Think of all the ways it is described to us. Composers have created marvelous songs. Painters and sculptors have tried to capture its meaning. Martyrs under persecution have clung to it. Christians find it a source of strength and healing in trying times.

The cross means more. It isn't only a lovely piece of art. It symbolizes all we believe in. It proclaims God's promise that we are set free from sin because Jesus died for us. It attests to the fact we really are saved by God's grace!

Think of the Lord Jesus who died on that cross. Take hold of His nail-pierced hands and don't let go. When darkness surrounds you and the earthquakes of life rumble like on the hill of Golgotha, know for sure that He has already provided the power to overcome anything and everything we face.

Call to remembrance the three crosses. Jesus hung on the center cross. He looked to one side and saw a thief who died an angry, unrepentant death. Jesus gazed at the man on the other side, another thief. This man begged for forgiveness and went on with Jesus to paradise.

See the cross in the center. The darkness is gone. Victory vibrates throughout the land. The veil in the temple has been split from top to bottom. No longer are we separated from the Holy of Holies! Death has been beaten!

All the crosses mankind has manufactured will perish. But the victory and power that came from God's love for us and Christ dying on that cross in the center shall never perish.

from *When I'm Praising God*
by ANITA CORRINE DONIHUE

THE SPIRIT OF CHRIST

And they that know thy name will put their trust in thee:
for thou, LORD, hast not forsaken them that seek thee.
PSALM 9:10

The crowd in the office seemed to have no morals whatsoever. Beth could hardly believe some of the things she heard the other employees talking about. They used foul language, spent weekends in drunken fogs, and had no compunction about their loose sexual behavior. Sometimes Beth felt so alone. It was hard to spend so much time out of the day with people she disagreed with so strongly. Her thoughts always turned to her close friends, and she was glad to have others who felt as she did to turn to. Her friends were all Christians, and it really did make a difference. She didn't feel like an outsider when she was with Christian friends. Having such good friends made it easier to deal with the people at work. She wondered what she would do if she didn't have friends who felt as she did.

So many people have no idea what it means to have the Spirit of Christ in their hearts. They believe that their lives are fine just as they are. How sad that they do not know enough to put their trust in God. It is our job, as the voice and hands of God, to let people know the truth of Christ, so they, too, might come to put their trust in Him.

∞

Make me an agent of Your will and Word. Help me to teach others by the example of my life what it means to be a Christian. I will put my trust in You. Help me to share that trust with others. Amen.

from *Wisdom from the Psalms*

Jesus in Gethsemane
(How to Enter In)

And he went a little farther,
and fell on his face, and prayed, saying,
O my Father, if it be possible, let this cup pass from me:
nevertheless not as I will, but as thou wilt.
MATTHEW 26:39

I was once trying to explain to a physician who had charge of a large hospital the necessity and meaning of consecration, but he seemed unable to understand. At last I said to him, "Suppose, in going your rounds among your patients, you should meet with one man who entreated you earnestly to take his case under your especial care in order to cure him, but who should at the same time refuse to tell you all his symptoms or to take all your prescribed remedies, and should say to you, 'I am quite willing to follow your directions as to certain things, because they commend themselves to my mind as good, but in other matters I prefer judging for myself, and following my own directions.' What would you do in such a case?" I asked.

"Do!" he replied with indignation, "I could do nothing for him unless he would put his whole case into my hands without any reserves, and would obey my directions implicitly."

"It is necessary, then," I said, "for doctors to be obeyed if they are to have any chance to cure their patient?"

"Implicitly obeyed!" was his emphatic reply.

"And that is consecration," I continued. "God must have the whole case put into His hands without any reserves."

from *The Christian's Secret of a Happy Life*
by HANNAH WHITALL SMITH

THE VIRTUOUS WOMAN

An excellent wife, who can find?
For her worth is far above jewels.
The heart of her husband trusts in her,
and he will have no lack of gain.
She does him good and not evil all the days of her life.

PROVERBS 31:10–12 NASB

When my husband was discharged from active duty with the army, we returned to California from Okinawa. We'd received a regular paycheck and housing allowance. Now we were thrust into an uncertain economy with a glut of civil engineers out of work. Consequently, my husband had to choose another major.

Dreams of evenings at home together spent with our growing family never materialized as my husband was either at his night school classes or in the library. The burden fell on my shoulders to keep our children occupied each night. We read books or worked on crafts together. At times, my days with the kids seemed endless, especially since none of them was yet in school.

After the little ones were finally tucked into bed, there were still a couple of hours before my bedraggled husband would reappear. I filled them with my own crafts, letter writing, reading, and Bible study.

The virtuous woman in the Scriptures did good to her husband and not evil. All her activities were geared toward building up her home. Through all those lonely hours, this is the example I followed. Years later, when my husband finally graduated with a degree in a new field, his family remained intact.

from *Daily Wisdom for Women*
by CAROL FITZPATRICK

His Appointments

Thy servants are ready to do whatsoever
my LORD the king shall appoint.
2 SAMUEL 15:15

I love to think that God appoints
My portion day by day;
Events of life are in His hand,
And I would only say,
Appoint them in Thine own good time,
And in Thine own best way.

A. L. WARING

If we are really, and always, and equally ready to do whatsoever the King appoints, all the trials and vexations arising from any change in His appointments, great or small, simply do not exist. If He appoints me to work there, shall I lament that I am not to work here? If He appoints me to wait indoors today, am I to be annoyed because I am not to work out-of-doors? If I meant to write His messages this morning, shall I grumble because He sends interrupting visitors, rich or poor, to whom I am to speak, or "show kindness" for His sake, or at least obey His command, "Be courteous"? If all my members are really at His disposal, why should I be put out if today's appointment is some simple work for my hands or errands for my feet, instead of some seemingly more important doing of head or tongue?

FRANCES RIDLEY HAVERGAL

compiled by MARY W. TILESTON

THE POWER OF GOD'S WORD

Therefore I say unto you, What things soever ye desire,
when ye pray, believe that ye receive them,
and ye shall have them.

MARK 11:24

The Holy Spirit's power is as great today as ever. Through prayer and Bible reading, we have the same victories available to us as Jesus did when He was raised from the dead. But trite prayer isn't enough. Fasting, praying, and praising make the difference.

The late 1800s were as difficult times as now. Sin lurked everywhere. Lives and families were destroyed. One of the most powerful preachers of that day saw all this firsthand. Here is a little of his timeless wisdom.

Thomas Guthrie shared effectively when he described the greatness of the Holy Spirit's power. He challenged Christians that in hell's hottest fires the devil never forged a plan that God's Spirit, wielding the hammer of His Word, couldn't strike out.

Doctor Guthrie passionately encouraged Christians to put the Bible to the test. Along with it, he urged everyone to call on the power of prayer. He told how the Bible, coupled with sincere wrestling and laboring, breaks the chains of sin and darkness.

He went on to impel us to step into the inner prison where Peter was brought forth by the angel's hands. At this point, we see the marvelous ways our prayers to God will be turned into victorious, grateful praises.

from *When I'm Praising God*
by ANITA CORRINE DONIHUE

Our Blessed Abundance

For the oppression of the poor,
for the sighing of the needy,
now will I arise,
saith the LORD.
PSALM 12:5

Something is terribly wrong in our world. Some of God's children are ill-fed, homeless, diseased, and abused. Many people do not know the comforts of a home, nor the security of a free state. Who will care for these lowly children of God?

The Bible says that the Lord will rise up in behalf of these people, but it also says that He will do so through His servants and followers. That means that God will provide for His poorer children through the grace of His richer ones. We are called to give from our blessed abundance, that others less fortunate might live. This is not an option for Christians, but a basic mandate upon which our faith is built. We are the hands, the feet, the eyes, and the voice of the Lord. Let us serve Him well.

∽

Use me as You will, O Lord. Make me an instrument of Thy glory and will. Send the power of Your Spirit into the world through me. Amen.

from *Wisdom from the Psalms*

HE LIVES!

I am he that liveth, and was dead;
and, behold, I am alive for evermore.

REVELATION 1:18

Flowers! Easter lilies! Speak to me this morning the same dear old lesson of immortality which you have been speaking to so many sorrowing souls.

Tree and blossom and bird and sea and sky and wind whisper it, sound it afresh, warble it, echo it, let it throb and pulsate through every atom and particle.

Let it be told and retold and still retold until hope rises to conviction, and conviction to certitude of knowledge; until we, like Paul, even though going to our death, go with triumphant mien, with assured faith, and with serene and shining face.

A well-known minister was in his study writing an Easter sermon when the thought gripped him that his Lord was *living*. He jumped up excitedly and paced the floor, repeating to himself, "Why, Christ is alive; His ashes are warm; He is not the great 'I was'; He is the great 'I am.'" He is not only a fact, but a *living* fact. Glorious truth of Easter Day!

We believe that out of every grave there blooms an Easter lily, and in every tomb there sits an angel. We believe in a risen Lord. Turn not your faces to the past that we may worship only at His grave, but above and within that we may worship the Christ that lives. And because He lives, we shall live also.

ABBOTT

from *Streams in the Desert*
by MRS. CHARLES E. COWMAN

In Memory of the Righteous

The memory of the righteous is blessed,
but the name of the wicked will rot.
PROVERBS 10:7 NASB

Not long ago, I attended the funeral of the mother of one of my husband's coworkers. Although I'd never met this man or his mother, knowing that his family had come from the Philippines drew me to the service. With their homeland so far away, perhaps there wouldn't be many in attendance.

Warmth, love, and appreciation greeted my husband and me from the moment we set foot in the chapel, which overflowed with guests. Somehow, this large family had assembled to provide a magnificent send-off for their precious "Nanay." Amid the battles of World War II, she was widowed at twenty-seven and left with three small children. Yet those difficult days of grief and hardship became her stepping-stones to faith in Christ. Later she remarried and was blessed with five more children.

Her parting admonition to the children who gathered around her deathbed was "be good and love each other." And then her Lord peacefully escorted her to the mansion He'd prepared.

This woman had lost so much. And yet, blessed with true wisdom, she turned to the Lord for solace and found in Him the foundation on which to build her life. To leave a rich legacy of love one must be dearly acquainted with the Author of Love, our heavenly Father.

from *Daily Wisdom for Women*
by CAROL FITZPATRICK

AS CLOSE AS A PRAYER

How long wilt thou forget me, O LORD? for ever?
how long wilt thou hide thy face from me?
PSALM 13:1

There is no worse feeling than feeling a distance from God. When we cry out in prayer, we need to feel His presence with us. When that feeling is absent, hopelessness and despair set in. We need to know, however, that the Lord has not really gone far from us, but we have pushed Him from ourselves. The Lord is always as close as a prayer, and we need to open our hearts to Him, and His presence will be felt once again. The Lord never hides His face from us, though often He will wait; stepping back like the loving Father that He is, to see whether or not we can struggle through a problem on our own. God wants to see us grow, and He often has to let us struggle a bit in order to allow that growth to occur. Even in those times of trial, however, the Lord is never far away, and He will not allow us to be tried beyond our endurance.

∞

Help me to know that You are with me in every situation at every moment of the day. I need Your comforting presence in my life, O Lord. Without it, I cannot go on. Amen.

from *Wisdom from the Psalms*

YOUR TRUST IN HIM

I am crucified with Christ: nevertheless I live;
yet not I, but Christ liveth in me:
and the life which I now live in the flesh
I live by the faith of the Son of God, who loved me,
and gave himself for me.
GALATIANS 2:20

Do you, then, now at this moment, surrender yourself wholly to Him? You answer, Yes. Then, my dear friend, begin at once to reckon that you are His, that He has taken you, and that He is working in you to will and to do of His good pleasure. And keep on reckoning this. You will find it a great help to put your reckoning into words, and say over and over to yourself and to your God, "Lord, I am Thine; I do yield myself up entirely to Thee, and I believe that Thou dost take me. I leave myself with Thee. Work in me all the good pleasure of Thy will, and I will only lie still in Thy hands and trust Thee."

Make this a daily, definite act of your will, and many times a day recur to it, as being your continual attitude before the Lord. Confess it to yourself. Confess it to your God. Confess it to your friends. Avouch the Lord to be your God, continually and unwaveringly, and declare your purpose of walking in His ways and keeping His statutes; and sooner or later, you will find in practical experience that He has avouched you to be one of His peculiar people, and will enable you to keep all of His commandments, and that you are being made into "an holy people unto the Lord, as he hath spoken."

from *The Christian's Secret of a Happy Life*
by HANNAH WHITALL SMITH

I Want to Leave My Mark for You

I press on toward the goal to win the prize for which God has called me heavenward in Christ Jesus.
PHILIPPIANS 3:14 NIV

I know not what each day holds, or what time I have left to serve. This I do know, dear Lord: I want to leave my mark for You.

Help me make every day count. Remind me to lay aside my own wants, to be willingly inconvenienced and used for You. Let me not put anything before You, no matter how good it seems. Help me shed bad habits that slow me down from doing Your will.

I can only leave my mark for You by replacing idle time with purposeful movement. When I rest, I open my heart that You may fill me with Your strength and spirit.

Teach me to let go of yesterday, live fully today, and look with excitement toward tomorrow. I am awed as I daily come to know You more. I feel You shower love upon me like a refreshing summer rain.

Even though I am unworthy, I long to reach the end of life's journey and see You face-to-face. In the meantime, Lord, may I use each day, each hour, each moment to leave my mark for You. Amen.

from *When I'm on My Knees*
by ANITA CORRINE DONIHUE

No Sense of Loyalty

Do not offer the parts of your body to sin,
as instruments of wickedness, but rather offer yourselves to God.
ROMANS 6:13 NIV

I hate my bathroom scale. It has no sense of loyalty whatsoever. I mean, all I did was overeat just a teensy bit last weekend, and it actually turned on me, claiming I had gained four pounds in three days. That's gratitude for you. I bought the scale in good faith. I placed it in a prominent place in the bathroom. I regularly replace the batteries to ensure complete accuracy. And now, with no warning at all, it mockingly flashes extra poundage at me.

The scale is obviously mistaken. I admit to savoring three pieces of my mom-in-law's world-famous chocolate pie, but I was standing up when I ate them. And we all know those calories don't count. I also sneaked a few items off Roy's tray when we went out Saturday night. But it's common knowledge that food originating from someone else's plate is completely void of calories or fat grams. And yes, I confess to inhaling a half-dozen doughnuts in one sitting. But that was only because I feared recrimination for leaving just two or three in the box. I had to eat them all in order to destroy the evidence that they ever existed in the first place.

So you see, the scale's claims are completely unfounded and irresponsible. But just as a precautionary measure, I plan to limit my snacking this week to low-cal popcorn. To help the taste, however, I'll need to use just a teensy-weensy bit of butter. . . .

from *Time Out*
by LEIGH ANN THOMAS

DEALING WITH ANNOYING PEOPLE

Judge not according to the appearance,
but judge righteous judgment.
JOHN 7:24

You forget perhaps the indirect good one may gain by living with uncongenial, tempting persons. . .such people do good by the very self-denial and self-control their mere presence demands."

"But suppose one cannot exercise self-control and is always flying out and flaring up?"

"I should say that a Christian who was always doing that. . .was in pressing need of just the trial God sent."

"It is very mortifying and painful to find how weak one is."

"That is true. But our mortifications are some of God's best physicians and do much toward healing our pride and self-conceit."

"We look at our fellowmen too much from the standpoint of our own prejudices. They may be wrong; they may have their faults and foibles; they may call out all the meanest and most hateful in us. But when they excite our bad passions by their own, they may be as ashamed and sorry as we are irritated. And I think some of the best, most contrite, most useful of men and women, whose prayers prevail with God and bring down blessings into the homes in which they dwell, often possess unlovely traits that furnish them with their best discipline. The very fact that they are ashamed of themselves drives them to God; they feel safe in His presence."

from *Stepping Heavenward*
by ELIZABETH PRENTISS

JUDGE YOURSELF

He that backbiteth not with his tongue, nor doeth evil to his neighbour, nor taketh up a reproach against his neighbour.
PSALM 15:3

Ruth attended every church function held, and she never refused to pitch in when there was work to do. She gave liberally of money, time, and talent. There was nothing she would not do for her church. Even so, she found that others did not welcome her or invite her to join in their special functions. One day she complained to the people she was with: "Too many people think too highly of themselves, and they're jealous of me because I do so much." She began to list by name those whom she meant. Finally, one of her associates stopped her and said, "The reason you're not more welcome is because you always talk about others. You spend a lot of time doing good, then you criticize people who don't do things like you want them to."

We are called to be Christian in thought, deed, and word. If the love of God truly dwells in our hearts, then we should show it by the way we treat and talk about others. What we say matters a great deal, and God will judge us on our words and feelings, as well as on our actions.

∞

Lord, help me to love with Your divine love. Keep me from judging others, but never let me forget that to grow, I must continually judge myself. Amen.

from *Wisdom from the Psalms*

TAKE COMFORT

For our light affliction, which is but for a moment,
worketh for us a far more exceeding and eternal weight of glory.
2 CORINTHIANS 4:17

Do you ever feel your trials are like wearing a crown of thorns? Be faithful. As you trust in God, your crown of thorns will be taken away, and He will hand you a crown with stars instead. Remember to thank and praise Him.

Do you feel like you are overloaded, your hands filled with heavy cares? Be faithful. As you keep trusting in God, He will take away your heavy cares and place a harp in your grasp, so you may sing glory and honor to God for all He has done. Remember to thank and praise Him.

Do your garments feel soiled with dirt and grime from struggling in a sin-sick world? Stay faithful. He will replace them with clothing that is shining white. Remember to thank and praise Him.

Hold on and do not despair. There will be a time when you look back and your trials will seem as nothing in light of the many answered prayers, miracles, and evidence of God's glory and grace.

Step by step, day by day, He takes each trial and turns it inside out. Triumphs emerge like a marvelous spiritual metamorphosis. Each of your obedient acts will be transformed to joy unspeakable!

So, take heart. Stay faithful. When all is ever so dark, know for sure morning follows the night.

When the dawn breaks through, remember to lift your heart in thanksgiving and praise to the One who gives all comfort and help.

from *When I'm Praising God*
by ANITA CORRINE DONIHUE

OF GROWTH

They shall mount up with wings as eagles.
ISAIAH 40:31

There is a fable about the way the birds got their wings at the beginning. They were first made without wings. Then God made the wings and put them down before the wingless birds and said to them, "Come, take up these burdens and bear them."

The birds had lovely plumage and sweet voices; they could sing, and their feathers gleamed in the sunshine, but they could not soar in the air. They hesitated at first when bidden to take up the burdens that lay at their feet, but soon they obeyed, and taking up the wings in their beaks, laid them on their shoulders to carry them.

For a little while the load seemed heavy and hard to bear, but presently, as they went on carrying the burdens; folding them over their hearts, the wings grew fast to their little bodies, and soon they discovered how to use them and were lifted by them up into the air—the weights became wings.

The fable is a parable. We are the wingless birds, and our duties and tasks are the pinions God has made to lift us up and carry us heavenward. We look at our burdens and heavy loads and shrink from them; but as we lift them and bind them about our hearts, they become wings; and on them we rise and soar toward God.

from *Streams in the Desert*
by MRS. CHARLES E. COWMAN

CONCERNING CONSECRATION

Thou hast avouched the LORD this day to be thy God,
and to walk in his ways, and to keep his statutes,
and his commandments, and his judgments,
and to hearken unto his voice.
DEUTERONOMY 26:17

E very devoted thing is most holy unto the LORD" (Leviticus 27:28). This is so plain as not to admit of a question.

But if the soul still feels in doubt or difficulty, let me refer you to a New Testament declaration which approaches the subject from a different side, but which settles it, I think, quite as definitely. It is in 1 John 5:14–15, and reads, "And this is the confidence that we have in him, that, if we ask any thing according to his will, he heareth us: and if we know that he hear us, whatsoever we ask, we know that we have the petitions that we desired of him." Is it according to His will that you would be entirely surrendered to Him? There can be, of course, but one answer to this, for He has commanded it. Is it not also according to His will that He should work in you to will and to do of His good pleasure? This question also can have but one answer, for He has declared it to be His purpose. You know, then, that these things are according to His will; therefore, on God's own Word, you are obliged to know that He hears you. And knowing this much, you are compelled to go farther, and know that you have the petitions that you have desired of Him.

from *The Christian's Secret of a Happy Life*
by HANNAH WHITALL SMITH

I Don't Like My Job

Whatever you do, work at it with all your heart,
as working for the LORD, not for men,
since you know that you will receive
an inheritance from the LORD as a reward.
It is the LORD Christ you are serving.
COLOSSIANS 3:23–24 NIV

Dear Father, I pray You will help me with my job. Things aren't going right. I dread going to work, and I need Your direction. On days I feel I'm doing more than my share, may my attitudes be right. Give me wisdom, I pray. When I do menial tasks, help me remember when Your Son, though King of kings, came down from heaven and often acted as a servant. Let me not be too proud to serve.

Help me to be honest in estimating my own abilities, to not put myself down or become a braggart. Teach me to appreciate a job well done, to feel an inner sense of accomplishment. I lean on You, not only on my skills. I know I can earn my pay and make a living; or I can give of myself and make a life.

Go before me when there is friction and backbiting. Let my motives be pure and uplifting, depending on Your help, so Your light can shine through.

from *When I'm on My Knees*
by ANITA CORRINE DONIHUE

INDIVIDUAL PATHS—ONE LIGHT

For as we have many members in one body,
and all members have not the same office:
so we, being many, are one body in Christ,
and every one members one of another.
ROMANS 12:4–5

During the nineteenth and twentieth centuries, the Stevenson family of Scotland was immersed in the lighthouse industry. They designed, built, and studied lighthouses, and they wrote many books dealing with navigational aids and lighthouse optics. Several members of the family became lighthouse engineers.

One of the members of this family was Robert Louis Stevenson, the author. The inspiration he drew from his family's lighthouses sent him in a different direction from the rest of his relatives. Although he did not become a lighthouse engineer as he had originally intended, he instead wrote the great seafaring classics, *Treasure Island* and *Kidnapped*.

We all do not follow Christ's light in the same manner. As we study His Word, we are each inspired to live out His love in individual ways. But we can be sure of this: His light is always the same, and when we follow Him, He will guide us all to life and safety.

from *A Beacon of Hope*
by ELLYN SANNA

A VEXATION ARISES

Let us not therefore judge one another any more:
but judge this rather,
that no man put a stumblingblock
or an occasion to fall in his brother's way.
ROMANS 14:13

My mind was ruffled with small cares today,
And I said pettish words, and did not keep
Long-suffering patience well, and now how deep
My trouble for this sin! In vain I weep
For foolish words I never can unsay.

H. S. SUTTON

A vexation arises, and our expressions of impatience hinder others from taking it patiently. Disappointment, ailment, or even weather depresses us; and our look or tone of depression hinders others from maintaining a cheerful and thankful spirit. We say an unkind thing, and another is hindered in learning the holy lessons of charity that thinks no evil. We say a provoking thing, and our sister or brother is hindered in that day's effort to be meek. How sadly, too, we may hinder without word or act! For wrong feeling is more infectious than wrongdoing; especially the various phases of ill temper—gloominess, touchiness, discontent, irritability—do we not know how catching these are?

FRANCES RIDLEY HAVERGAL

compiled by MARY W. TILESTON

Knowing God

In the beginning was the Word,
and the Word was with God,
and the Word was God.

John 1:1

To know God, therefore, as He really is, we must go to His incarnation in the Lord Jesus Christ. The Bible tells us that no man has seen God at any time, but that the only begotten Son of the Father, He has revealed Him. When one of the disciples said to Christ, "Shew us the Father, and it sufficeth us," Christ answered, "Have I been so long time with you, and yet hast thou not known me, Philip? he that hath seen me hath seen the Father, and how sayest thou then, Shew us the Father? Believest thou not that I am in the Father, and the Father in me? the words that I speak unto you I speak not of myself: but the Father that dwelleth in me, he doeth the works" (John 14:8–10).

Here then is our opportunity. We cannot see God, but we can see Christ. Christ was not only the Son of God, but He was the Father. Whatever Christ was, that God is. All the unselfishness, all the tenderness, all the kindness, all the justice, and all the goodness that we see in Christ is simply a revelation of the unselfishness, the tenderness, the kindness, the justice, and the goodness of God.

Someone has said lately, in words that seem to me inspired, "Christ is the human form of God." And this is the explanation of the Incarnation.

by Hannah Whitall Smith

CONTENTMENT

I have learned, in whatsoever state I am,
therewith to be content.
PHILIPPIANS 4:11

Paul, denied of every comfort, wrote the above words in his dungeon. A story is told of a king who went into his garden one morning and found everything withered and dying. He asked the oak that stood near the gate what the trouble was. He found it was sick of life and determined to die because it was not tall and beautiful like the pine. The pine was all out of heart because it could not bear grapes like the vine. The vine was going to throw its life away because it could not stand erect and have as fine fruit as the peach tree; and so on all through the garden. Coming to a heartsease, he found its bright face lifted as cheery as ever. "Well, heartsease, I'm glad, amidst all this discouragement, to find one brave little flower. You do not seem to be the least disheartened." "No, I am not of much account, but I thought that if you wanted an oak, or a pine, or a peach tree, or a lilac, you would have planted one; but as I knew you wanted a heartsease, I am determined to be the best little heartsease that I can."

They who are God's without reserve, are in every state content; for they will only what He wills, and desire to do for Him whatever He desires them to do; they strip themselves of everything, and in this nakedness find all things restored an hundredfold.

from *Streams in the Desert*
by MRS. CHARLES E. COWMAN

MAKE ROOM FOR PEACE

Let us lay aside every weight,
. . .let us run with patience the race that is set before us.
HEBREWS 12:1

O ur society is a busy one. As we dash from responsibility to responsibility, we seem to pride ourselves on our busyness, as though it somehow proves our worth. Even our children are busy, their schedules crammed with enriching activities. We all fly through life, fitting as many things as we can into each day.

With such complicated lives, it's no wonder we find our hearts craving quiet. We long for it so much that books on peace and simplicity climb the best-seller lists; we're all hoping some author will have the magic answer that will show us how to infuse our lives with serenity.

But we're looking at peace as though it were one more thing to fit into our lives, as though we could write it on our to-do list. (There it is, right between *Take the dog to the vet* and *Pick up the clothes from the dry cleaner. Find a little peace.*) But the truth is, that's not the way peace works.

The only way we will find peace in the midst of our hectic lives is if we make room for it. When we stop the mad rush, when we say no to some of our many responsibilities and take the time to come quietly into God's presence, then, in that simple, quiet moment, He will breathe His peace into our hearts.

from *Keep It Simple*
by ELLYN SANNA

I WON'T WORRY FOR THE FUTURE

"Who of you by worrying can add a single hour to his life?
Since you cannot do this very little thing,
why do you worry about the rest?"
LUKE 12:25–26 NIV

Sometimes I feel overwhelmed, wondering what the future holds. Then I remember that worry and fear are not from You. I praise You, Lord, for having control of my future.

Why should I be anxious over what tomorrow or the next day brings when I'm Your child and You have my needs and best interests at heart? Thank You for caring for me, not only now but always. Thank You for caring for those I love. I trust You that now—and even someday when I leave this perishable body and join You in heaven—You will be answering my prayers for my loved ones down through generations.

I read of how, although Abraham's faith was strong, sometimes he doubted Your promises for his future. Sometimes he created disasters by taking things into his own hands. In spite of all that, You still blessed him and Sarah in their later years with a wonderful son.

You have authority over all, so I will not worry for the future. I will trust in You with all my heart and I won't depend on my own understanding. Instead, in all my ways I'll be in tune with You and Your will to guide and direct my paths.

Thank You for the future, Lord. I praise You for going before me and making a way.

from *When I'm Praising God*
by ANITA CORRINE DONIHUE

THE UNFORGIVABLE SIN

*"And I say to you, everyone who confesses Me before men,
the Son of Man shall confess him also before the angels of God;
but he who denies Me before men shall be denied
before the angels of God."*
LUKE 12:8–9 NASB

When I was growing up, life seemed simple. For instance, as a child I learned there were mortal and venial sins. Venial sins could be forgiven; mortal sins guaranteed that your one-way ticket to heaven would never get punched.

However, God says that if we're guilty of breaking one part of the law, then we're guilty of breaking the entire law. So, what hope do any of us have?

Well, God built in a fail-safe. As the disciples celebrated the Feast of Pentecost, God fulfilled His promise to send the Holy Spirit (Acts 2:1–4). God's Spirit filled the apostles, compelling them to preach the Gospel in every language of that day, that all might hear the truth (Acts 2:11).

All men are in need of a Savior. And the Bible states clearly that only one person fills this job description. "And there is salvation in no one else; for there is no other name under heaven that has been given among men, by which we must be saved" (Acts 4:12 NASB). Jesus Christ is that Savior.

The only sin that has the power to place you on the wrong side of heaven is one of neglect. If you refuse to be "born again" of God's Spirit (John 3:5–7), you will not be received in heaven (Mark 3:29).

from *Daily Wisdom for Women*
by CAROL FITZPATRICK

FATIGUE

For which cause we faint not;
but though our outward man perish,
yet the inward man is renewed day by day.
2 CORINTHIANS 4:16

Let my soul beneath her load
Faint not through the o'erwearied flesh;
Let me hourly drink afresh
Love and peace from Thee, my God!

RICHTER

In my attempts to promote the comfort of my family, the quiet of my spirit has been disturbed. Some of this is doubtless owing to physical weakness; but, with every temptation, there is a way of escape; there is never any need to sin. Another thing I have suffered loss from—entering into the business of the day without seeking to have my spirit quieted and directed. So many things press upon me, this is sometimes neglected; shame to me that it should be so.

This is of great importance, to watch carefully—now I am so weak—not to overfatigue myself, because then I can not contribute to the pleasure of others; and a placid face and a gentle tone will make my family more happy than anything else I can do for them. Our own will gets sadly into the performance of our duties sometimes.

ELIZABETH T. KING

compiled by MARY W. TILESTON

STRONG IN HIS LOVE

He teacheth my hands to war,
so that a bow of steel is broken by mine arms.
PSALM 18:34

Angela was the youngest of six children. Her memories of childhood conjured images of constant fighting and competition. She had learned very early how to fight. Her young years had been a painful lesson in the survival of the fittest.

It was only after she left home that she found out that living didn't mean fighting. She met and married a strong Christian man whose strength came not from any physical source, but from a deep and abiding faith in the Lord. He taught her patience and compassion and peace. Her world was turned upside down as she realized that true strength came not from fighting, but from refusing to fight. God granted her a power greater than any she'd known. By her peace of mind and spirit, Angela broke free from the bondage of her past and faced the future with the assurance that nothing could ever defeat her again.

∞

Lord, remove from me my spirit of competition in trying to be better than other people. Whenever my will says to fight back in anger, let my spirit prevail with a desire to forgive. Make me strong in Your love. Amen.

from *Wisdom from the Psalms*

SAY "YES" TO GOD

Teach me to do thy will; for thou art my God:
thy spirit is good;
lead me into the land of uprightness.
PSALM 143:10

Have you come to a fork in your road of life? Do you feel God's call to serve? Do you recognize His voice and know it is Him? Simply wait on Him and say, "Yes."

Don't ponder over the what-ifs or whys, neither question your abilities. Don't worry about timing or the future. Test the calling to be sure it is of God. When you know it is Him, simply tell Him, "Yes."

When the mighty winds blow, He will miraculously place them at your back. When the floods begin to rage, He may tell you to keep paddling in faith, believing, while He calms the seas.

God's calling is sure. We don't have to worry about making a way. If it is His will, He works all things out in His own perfect way and timing.

He calls us through, around, over, and under to serve. No foe can stop us; no poverty can starve us; no evil can diminish His call. For He has a glorious plan!

So, just say, "Yes."

from *When I'm Praising God*
by ANITA CORRINE DONIHUE

THE GREAT SCANDAL

What shall we say then?
Shall we continue in sin,
that grace may abound?

ROMANS 6:1

Can we, for a moment, suppose that the holy God, who hates sin in the sinner, is willing to tolerate it in the Christian, and that He has even arranged the plan of salvation in such a way as to make it impossible for those who are saved from the guilt of sin to find deliverance from its power?

As Dr. Chalmers well says, "Sin is that scandal which must be rooted out from the great spiritual household over which the Divinity rejoices. Strange administration, indeed, for sin to be so hateful to God as to lay all who had incurred it under death, and yet, when readmitted into life, that sin should be permitted; and that what was before the object of destroying vengeance should now become the object of an upheld and protected toleration. Now that the penalty is taken off, think you it is possible that the unchangeable God has so given up His antipathy to sin as that man, ruined and redeemed man, may now perseveringly indulge, under the new arrangement, in that which under the old destroyed him? Does not the God who loved righteousness and hated iniquity six thousand years ago bear the same love to righteousness and hatred to iniquity still?"

from *The Christian's Secret of a Happy Life*
by HANNAH WHITALL SMITH

MOTIVES OF THE HEART

*The plans of the heart belong to man, but the answer of the tongue
is from the Lord. All the ways of a man are clean in his own sight,
but the LORD weighs the motives. Commit your works to the
LORD, And your plans will be established. The LORD has made
everything for its own purpose, even the wicked for the day of evil.*
PROVERBS 16:1–4 NASB

Horoscopes in newspapers and psychic telephone hotlines
exist because people have a natural curiosity to know the
future. Despite the phenomenal success of recent Hollywood
blockbusters, I can assure you an attack by aliens is not on
the horizon. No, our real threat will come from within the
very real but unseen spiritual realm, not the extraterrestrial.

You've heard the expression, "Men are from Mars and
women are from Venus." But the Bible does not distinguish
between the hearts of men and women: "The heart is more
deceitful than all else and is desperately sick; who can understand it?" (Jeremiah 17:9 NASB)

Surrounding us are beings from another world, but they
belong to Satan. And their sole purpose is to seduce us into
wavering from the truth. They dangle and then entangle us
from the scaffolding of unbelief. Did God mean what He
said? Doesn't He want us to have any fun? Do we really need
Him telling us what to do? Absolutely! Only God can give
us a secure, peaceful, and perfect future—an eternal future in
heaven with Him.

∞

*Lord, there have been times when I compromised the truth of your
Word. Please help me get back on track. Place my feet firmly on the
pavement of Your Word.*

from *Daily Wisdom for Women*
by CAROL FITZPATRICK

Healthy Fear

The fear of the LORD is clean, enduring for ever:
the judgments of the LORD are true and righteous altogether.
PSALM 19:9

Patty always laughed whenever anyone tried to tell her that what she did was sinful. She would mock her friends, telling them they sounded like old ladies. Gwen couldn't understand how Patty could do the things she did and still call herself a Christian. Gwen was surprised to see Patty standing at her door in tears.

Patty had begun to wake up to the fact that she really was living a wrong lifestyle. The more she thought about it, the worse she felt. She hoped that Gwen could help her. Gwen told her that she was already on the right track to finding help. Realizing that what you do is wrong is the first step. Fearing what might happen because of what you do is the next step. Fear can be a healthy thing for us when it forces us to clean up our lives and walk the straight path. Once on the right path, we can leave fear behind, for nothing can harm us once we are in the Lord's camp. God's judgments are righteous and true, and He will always help us make the changes that allow us to clean up our lives, if we will only ask Him to.

∞

I need to respect You more, Lord. I need to be reminded that Your way is the only way, so that I won't be so tempted to stray. Be with me to guide me. Amen.

from *Wisdom from the Psalms*

CHRIST, OUR YOKEFELLOW

Take my yoke upon you, and learn of me; for I am meek and lowly in heart: and ye shall find rest unto your souls.
MATTHEW 11:29

We read how in ages past our ancestors used workhorses, oxen, and mules for means of transportation and heavy labor. They must not have taken long to discover that two or more animals had trouble working and pulling together. But a yoke carefully placed over a pair of the animals' shoulders helped them to pull together.

Slaves and prisoners shared yokes. In every situation, the yoke made the work stronger and more efficient.

Much later, brilliant people came up with the idea of automobiles. They invented parts of an engine that depend on each other in the same way. They found out how to make compression build up in the head by piston strokes, how to transfer the energy by rocker arms, rods, etc., to a crankshaft, then to the wheels.

Sometimes, when two people are united as one, they use the words "putting on a yoke" to express their unity. In so doing, each one is known as a yokefellow: an intimate associate, partner, or spouse.

When Jesus tells us to take His yoke upon us so our burden will be light, I wonder if He is offering to be our blessed Yokefellow, to lead and guide us through our daily lives.

As we let Him take control, we become one with Him. It is amazing how much easier our burdens become.

from *When I'm Praising God*
by ANITA CORRINE DONIHUE

BELIEVE YOUR FATHER

Jesus answered and said unto them,
Verily I say unto you, If ye have faith, and doubt not,
ye shall not only do this which is done to the fig tree,
but also if ye shall say unto this mountain,
Be thou removed, and be thou cast into the sea; it shall be done.
MATTHEW 21:21

You are no more under a necessity to be doubtful as to your relationship to your heavenly Father than you are to be doubtful as to your relationship to your earthly father. In both cases the thing you must depend on is their word, not your feelings; and no earthly father has ever declared or manifested his fatherhood one thousandth part as unmistakably or as lovingly as your heavenly Father has declared and manifested His. If you would not "make God a liar," therefore, you must make your believing as inevitable and necessary a thing as your obedience. You would obey God, I believe, even though you should die in the act. Believe Him, also, even though the effort to believe should cost you your life. The conflict may be very severe; it may seem at times unendurable. But let your unchanging declaration be from henceforth, "Though he slay me, yet will I trust in him" (Job 13:15). When doubts come, meet them, not with arguments, but with assertions of faith. All doubts are an attack of the enemy; the Holy Spirit never suggests them, never. He is the Comforter, not the Accuser; and He never shows us our need without at the same time revealing the divine supply.

from *The Christian's Secret of a Happy Life*
by HANNAH WHITALL SMITH

A Mother's Influence

Teach your children to choose the right path,
and when they are older,
they will remain upon it.
PROVERBS 22:6, NLT

If my mother had been a different woman, I would be a different person. When she read to me each night, I learned about the world of words; today I make my living writing—and I still love coming home from the library with a stack of books to keep me company. When my mother took me outdoors and named the trees and flowers and birds for me, I learned about the world of nature; today, whenever I'm upset or discouraged, I still find peace walking in the woods, and when I recognize ash and beech, trilliums and hepatic, purple finches and indigo buntings, I feel as though I'm saying the names of dear, old friends. And when my mother prayed with me each night and before each meal, I learned about an eternal world; today I seek God's presence daily and offer up my life to Him in prayer.

My mother trained me well.

from *Just the Girls*
by ELLYN SANNA

Seek Wisdom, Not Self

When a wicked man comes, contempt also comes,
and with dishonor comes reproach.

PROVERBS 18:3 NASB

The delightful movie *Doctor Doolittle* presented a magical animal called the "Push me, pull you." Such is the woman who has a divided heart! She can never truly go forward in life.

One young woman whom I counseled certainly fit this description. She'd fallen in love with a worthless wretch of a man and become convinced that she somehow possessed the power to change him. Not only could she not change him, she was also unable to raise her children properly. Because this mother was emotionally paralyzed, her children never received godly examples of faith, integrity, and stability.

Women become vulnerable the instant truth is replaced with desire. It's like when the tip of an arrow finds the one small point of vulnerability and penetrates a suit of armor.

So how can we teach our daughters to be wise? By acquiring knowledge ourselves. As we study and store God's Word in times of peace, our first thoughts during periods of stress or crisis will be Scripture. People falter because they fail to plan. If we just do what God expects of us, despite the magnetic pull of sin, we gain strength of character. Negotiating with evil nets us a zero every time.

∞

Lord, sometimes I want so badly to be loved that I trust the wrong people. Please guide me to those who are trustworthy.

from *Daily Wisdom for Women*
by CAROL FITZPATRICK

HE IS ALTOGETHER LOVELY

His mouth is most sweet: yea, he is altogether lovely.
This is my beloved, and this is my friend,
O daughters of Jerusalem.
SONG OF SOLOMON 5:16

It is not when we are following afar off that we find Jesus Christ "altogether lovely"; it is not when we are flirting with the world, nor when we are compromising the truth of the gospel, that we experience the sweetness of His mouth. It is when we draw close to Him and follow hard after Him; when we constrain Him to come in and sup with us, and we with Him, that we exclaim: "His aspect is like Lebanon, excellent as the cedars. His mouth is most sweet." It is when all else has faded away into insignificance, and He alone fills our vision, that we apprehend the sweetness of His love, which can only be revealed to us as we enter into this place of separation.

It is as we set our faces to know Him; it is as we go through the keenest suffering and persecution for His dear sake, in order to receive all He has for us, that He is altogether lovely. Only as we are without the gate can our eyes be anointed with heavenly eye salve; only as our eyes are anointed by the Holy Spirit can we see Him clearly. Then do we realize that there is none else who is lovely; and to us, none other is desirable and delightful.

by CORA HARRIS MACILRAVY

SEASONS

To every thing there is a season,
and a time to every purpose under the heaven.
ECCLESIASTES 3:1

B ob and I broke away from responsibilities and took a drive to our favorite place, the ocean, for a couple of days. After a brief night's sleep, I awakened early.

No matter how tired I am, I can't resist waking before dawn and walking out to a nearby jetty. This morning was no different. I quietly slipped into warm clothes and shoes. Bob already knew where I would go. Before long, my strides lengthened and quickened. I approached the pier.

Responsibilities had been crashing in on my life harder than the breakers hitting the huge rocks before me. I watched the waves roll in. They crashed, sprayed, and flowed out over and over in rhythmic patterns, then prepared to do it again.

"Lord, why must I be stretched so thin? I don't think I can handle it all much longer," I whispered.

The sun peeked above the ocean and reflected its rays across the waves.

Peace, be still, I felt God whisper on the wind. *Look at the tide change. It's going out now. To everything there is a time and a season. The hard toil won't last forever. In the meantime—rest.*

God reminded me to praise Him while I watched the waves recede. Cold air rushed about me, but warmth filled my being. His presence comforted, assured me.

"Thank You, God, for the seasons," I prayed. I turned, set a quick pace, and headed toward rest, a hot cup of tea, and my waiting beloved. I had been blessed.

from *When I'm Praising God*
by ANITA CORRINE DONIHUE

Acquaintance with God

But we have this treasure in earthen vessels,
that the excellency of the power may be of God, and not of us.
2 Corinthians 4:7

Who could have anything but peace in coming to know that the God who has created us, and to whom we belong forever, is a God of love? And what else is there that can bring an unwavering peace?

Acquaintance with doctrines or dogmas may give peace for a time, or blissful experience may, or success in service; but the peace from these can never be trusted to abide. Doctrines may become obscure; experiences may be dulled or may change; we may be cut off by providential circumstances from our work; all things and all people may seem to fail us. The only place, therefore, of permanent and abiding peace is to be found in an acquaintance with the goodness and the unselfishness of God.

In human relations we may know a great deal about a person without at all necessarily coming into any actual acquaintance with that person; and it is the same in our relations with God. We may blunder on for years thinking we know a great deal about Him, but never quite sure of what sort of Being He actually is, and consequently never finding any permanent rest or satisfaction. And then, perhaps suddenly, we catch a sight of Him as He is revealed in the face of Jesus Christ, and we discover the real God. We no longer need His promises; we have found Himself, and He is enough for every need.

by Hannah Whitall Smith

Diamonds in the Rough

The secret of the LORD is with them that fear him.
PSALM 25:14

There are secrets of Providence which God's dear children may learn. His dealings with them often seem, to the outward eye, dark and terrible. Faith looks deeper and says, "This is God's secret. You look only on the outside; I can look deeper and see the hidden meaning."

Sometimes diamonds are done up in rough packages, so that their value cannot be seen.

God may send you, dear friends, some costly packages. Do not worry if they are done up in rough wrappings. You may be sure there are treasures of love, and kindness, and wisdom hidden within. If we take what He sends, and trust Him for the goodness in it, even in the dark, we shall learn the meaning of the secrets of Providence.

A. B. SIMPSON

He that is mastered by Christ is the master of every circumstance. Does the circumstance press hard against you? Do not push it away. It is the Potter's hand. Your mastery will come, not by arresting its progress, but by enduring its discipline, for it is not only shaping you into a vessel of beauty and honor, but it is making your resources available.

from *Streams in the Desert*
by MRS. CHARLES E. COWMAN

A Long, Slow Journey

For that which I do I allow not: for what I would,
that do I not; but what I hate, that do I.
ROMANS 7:15

Once my heart responds to God's love, I quickly become discouraged by my own sinful nature. In moments of emotion, I promise myself that I will certainly fly straight to heaven—but all too soon, I return to the ordinary difficulties of daily life. I am disappointed to find that I am just as self-ish and easily irritated, just as full of pride and impatience as ever. My progress toward heaven goes in fits and spurts.

But these fluctuations in the spiritual life are normal. I cannot make myself holy, any more than I could give myself eternal life. Both those things are Christ's job—and as I give myself to Christ moment by moment, day after day, His redeeming power continues to work in my life, making me whole.

from *Stepping Heavenward*
by ELIZABETH PRENTISS

Lowly Work

*These were the potters, and those that dwelt among plants
and hedges: there they dwelt with the king for his work.*
1 Chronicles 4:23

A lowlier task on them is laid,
With love to make the labor light;
And there their beauty they must shed
On quiet homes, and lost to sight.
Changed are their visions high and fair,
Yet, calm and still, they labor there.

Hymns of the Ages

Anywhere and everywhere we may dwell "with the King for His work." We may be in a very unlikely or unfavorable place for this; it may be in a literal country life, with little enough to be seen of the "goings" of the King around us; it may be among hedges of all sorts, hindrances in all directions; it may be furthermore, with our hands full of all manner of pottery for our daily task. No matter! The King who placed us "there" will come and dwell there with us; the hedges are all right, or He would soon do away with them; and it does not follow that what seems to hinder our way may not be for its very protection; and as for the pottery, why, that is just exactly what he has seen fit to put into our hands, and therefore it is, for the present, "His work."

Frances Ridley Havergal

compiled by Mary W. Tileston

What Is Prayer?

O my God, I cry in the daytime, but thou hearest not;
and in the night season, and am not silent.

PSALM 22:2

Prayer is a tricky thing. It was never meant as a "gimme" list by which we can get things from God. It is not a gripe time to vent frustrations and woes. It is not a time to show off our piety. Rather, it is a time to draw close to God in order to be open to His will and guidance. So often we feel that God is not listening because we don't get what we ask for. We want results immediately, and we decide beforehand what we will accept as an answer and what we will not. Who says we get to make the rules? The Lord hears us, and He is true to answer us, but He always measures His responses according to His divine wisdom. He knows what is best for us, even when it doesn't agree with what we want. It is natural and human to doubt the Lord sometimes. He understands that. Just don't give up. The Lord breaks through our desert spots, to comfort us when we cry.

∞

Lift me, Lord, into Your loving arms. Grace me with the sweet memory of Your care, that I might never doubt You in times of trial. Amen.

from *Wisdom from the Psalms*

How to Enter In

But thou, when thou prayest, enter into thy closet,
and when thou hast shut thy door,
pray to thy Father which is in secret;
and thy Father which seeth in secret shall reward thee openly.
MATTHEW 6:6

A Christian lady who had this feeling was once expressing to a friend how impossible she found it to say, "Thy will be done," and how afraid she should be to do it. She was the mother of an only little boy who was the heir to a great fortune and the idol of her heart. After she had stated her difficulties fully, her friend said, "Suppose your little Charley should come running to you tomorrow and say, 'Mother, I have made up my mind to let you have your own way with me from this time forward. I am always going to obey you, and I want you to do just whatever you think best with me. I will trust your love.' How would you feel towards him? Would you say to yourself, 'Ah, now I shall have a chance to make Charley miserable. I will take away all his pleasures, and fill his life with every hard and disagreeable thing that I can find. I will compel him to do just the things that are the most difficult for him to do, and will give him all sorts of impossible commands.' "

"Oh, no, no, no!" exclaimed the indignant mother. "You know I would not. You know I would hug him to my heart and cover him with kisses, and would hasten to fill his life with all that was sweetest and best."

"And are you more tender and more loving than God?"

from *The Christian's Secret of a Happy Life*
by HANNAH WHITALL SMITH

CALLED TO GREATER SEPARATION

Thou hast ravished my heart, my sister, my spouse;
thou hast ravished my heart with one of thine eyes,
with one chain of thy neck.
SONG OF SOLOMON 4:9

Precious Savior! How oft have we heard Thee knocking at the doors of our hearts; not only when we were sinners, but even after we had tasted and knew that the Lord was good, and had proved Thine infinite love.

How dull we are when it comes to a realization of the love of Christ. We are like little children who watch the beautiful colors and dazzling lights in a priceless diamond, but know not its value. We have no conception of what it cost our Lord to purchase redemption for mankind; we know not His suffering. We shall never know the anguish that broke His heart as He hung on the cross, deserted by all who had claimed to love Him.

Oh, that we might love Him more! It seems that He demands so little from us in comparison with what He has given us. Even a little turning of our love toward Him, and His heart responds to us, and the warmth of His love sweeps over us like flaming billows. Even a little turning of our faces toward Him with determination to go on into all He has bought for us, and He hastens to meet us.

by CORA HARRIS MACILRAVY

PRAYING FOR OTHERS

Deliver my soul from the sword;
my darling from the power of the dog.
PSALM 22:20

Perhaps the most pleasing prayer that we offer to God is the prayer that we pray for someone else. A prayer for another person is an unselfish and caring act. It takes the trust we have in God and extends it outward in behalf of other people. It is an example of how we can walk in the footsteps of Jesus. Certainly, God wants us to pray for our personal needs, but we enter into His ministry and love when we send forth our prayers in the names of others.

∞

Hear the concerns of my heart, Almighty God. I care for so many people, and I want to lift them up to Your care. Be with them and give them the blessings that You continue to give to me. Make Yourself real in their lives, Lord. Amen.

from *Wisdom from the Psalms*

C. J. AND THE CAT

Bless the LORD, O my soul: and all that is within me,
bless his holy name.
PSALM 103:1

Ten-year-old C. J. had been in my Sunday school class for two years. I knew him well. One Sunday morning he shared a prayer request with us. He wanted prayer for his sick cat. I lightheartedly added the request to several others as we prayed.

The next Sunday C. J. told how his cat was getting worse and the veterinarian was concerned about the cat's recovery. It came time for morning worship service. When my husband, Bob, asked for prayer requests, C. J. raised his hand and asked for prayer for his cat.

Bob looked surprised. Some people smiled. Others stifled chuckles. Bob gingerly added C. J.'s request to several others, asking that God would be with C. J.

After church, C. J. came to me. "I want us to pray for my cat, not me," he announced.

At that moment, God spoke to my heart. The two of us sat on the back pew in the sanctuary and prayed earnestly for God to heal C. J.'s cat. Then I turned to my dear student and told him to tell everyone he had prayed for his cat and to give God the praise.

What am I saying? I wondered. *Lord, this is really putting our prayers to the test.*

The next week in Sunday school class C. J. said the cat was recovering. Our class thanked God together.

Later that day, I praised God again for the unexpected little blessing of C. J. and his cat.

from *When I'm Praising God*
by ANITA CORRINE DONIHUE

GOD IS REAL

Now faith is the substance of things hoped for,
the evidence of things not seen.
HEBREWS 11:1

Because God is not visibly present to the eye, it is difficult to feel that a transaction with Him is real. I suppose that if, when we made our acts of consecration, we could actually see Him present with us, we should feel it to be a very real thing, and would realize that we had given our word to Him, and could not dare to take it back, no matter how much we might wish to do so. Such a transaction would have to us the binding power that a spoken promise to an earthly friend always has to a man of honor. What we need, therefore, is to see that God's presence is a certain fact always, and that every act of our soul is done before Him, and that a word spoken in prayer is as really spoken to Him as if our eyes could see Him and our hands could touch Him. Then we shall cease to have such vague conceptions of our relations with Him, and shall feel the binding force of every word we say in His presence.

from *The Christian's Secret of a Happy Life*
by HANNAH WHITALL SMITH

Sailing by Faith

He went out, not knowing whither he went.
HEBREWS 11:8

When we can see, it is not faith, but reasoning. In crossing the Atlantic, we observed this very principle of faith. We saw no path upon the sea, nor sign of the shore. And yet day by day we were marking our path upon the chart as exactly as if there had followed us a great chalk line upon the sea. And when we came within twenty miles of land, we knew where we were as exactly as if we had seen it all three thousand miles ahead.

How had we measured and marked our course? Day by day our captain had taken his instruments and, looking up to the sky, had fixed his course by the sun. He was sailing by the heavenly, not the earthly, lights.

So faith looks up and sails on, by God's great Sun, not seeing one shoreline or earthly lighthouse or path upon the way. Often its steps seem to lead into utter uncertainty, and even darkness and disaster; but He opens the way, and often makes such midnight hours the very gates of day. Let us go forth this day, not knowing, but trusting.

Waiting on God brings us to our journey's end quicker than our feet.

from *Streams in the Desert*
by MRS. CHARLES E. COWMAN

A Long, Slow Journey

Knowing this,
that our old man is crucified with him,
that the body of sin might be destroyed,
that henceforth we should not serve sin.

ROMANS 6:6

Make your complaint, tell Him how obscure everything still looks to you, and beg Him to complete your cure. He may see fit to try your faith and patience by delaying this completion; but meanwhile you are safe in His presence, and while led by His hand, He will excuse the mistakes you make and pity your falls. But you will imagine that it is best that He should enable you at once to see clearly. If it is, you may be sure He will do it. He never makes mistakes. But He often deals far differently with His disciples. He lets them grope their way in the dark until they fully learn how blind they are, how helpless, how absolutely in need of Him.

from *Stepping Heavenward*
by ELIZABETH PRENTISS

INTERRUPTIONS

The LORD thy God shall bless thee in all thy works,
and in all that thou puttest thine hand unto.
DEUTERONOMY 15:10

My place of lowly service, too,
Beneath Thy sheltering wings I see;
For all the work I have to do
Is done through sheltering rest in Thee.

A. L. WARING

I think I find most help in trying to look on all interruptions
and hindrances to work that one has planned out for one-
self as discipline, trials sent by God to help one against getting selfish over one's work. Then one can feel that perhaps
one's true work—one's work for God—consists in doing
some trifling haphazard thing that has been thrown into one's
day. It is not waste of time, as one is tempted to think. It is
the most important part of the work of the daythe part one
can best offer to God. After such a hindrance, do not rush
after the planned work; trust that the time to finish it will be
given sometime, and keep a quiet heart about it.

ANNIE KEARY

compiled by MARY W. TILESTON

PEACE LIKE A RIVER

The LORD is my shepherd;
I shall not want.
He maketh me to lie down in green pastures:
he leadeth me beside the still waters.
PSALM 23:1–2

I like the word serenity. It always seems to me to be a shining word, like sunlight glimmering on quiet water. When I was small, I thought that serene people carried a deep well of peace in them; I imagined I could see the cool, still water that flowed out of them, refreshing and quieting the dusty, noisy crowds around them.

I'm not the only one who connects serenity with water. The Bible also speaks of peace being like a quiet river. And David writes of the Shepherd who leads us beside the still, calm waters, quieting our hearts.

Obviously, there's a connection between serenity and water. After all, they both refresh us; they both give us life. And they both help to wash us clean of the ordinary grime and dust that darken our lives.

For in the quiet moments when we draw away from the noise and bustle of human life, we come into God's presence. Alone with Him, we open our hearts—and we are restored, brought back to life, washed clean. His Spirit speaks peace to our hearts.

And as we go back to the noise and the hurry, we can choose to carry His Spirit with us, a deep, quiet well of serenity in our hearts.

from *Keep It Simple*
by ELLYN SANNA

SOUL FOOD

Wherefore do ye spend money for that which is not bread?
and your labour for that which satisfieth not?
hearken diligently unto me, and eat ye that which is good,
and let your soul delight itself in fatness.
ISAIAH 55:2

G ive us this day our daily bread," is a prayer that includes the soul as well as the body, and unless the religion of Christ contains this necessary food for our weekday lives, as well as for our Sunday lives, it is a grievous failure. But this it does. It is full of principles that fit into human life, as it is in its ordinary commonplace aspects; and the soul that would grow strong must feed itself on these, as well as on the more dainty fare of sermons and services and weekly celebrations.

Does not plain common sense teach us that when people feed their souls upon a diet of gossip or of frivolities of any kind, they must necessarily suffer from languor of spiritual life, debility of spiritual digestion, failure of vitality, and a creeping moral paralysis?

"But lusted exceedingly in the wilderness, and tempted God in the desert. And he gave them their request; but sent leanness into their soul" (Psalm 106:14–15).

"Leanness of soul" arises far more often than we think from the indigestible nature of the spiritual food we have been feeding upon.

by HANNAH WHITALL SMITH

Praying Patiently

Rest in the LORD, and wait patiently for him.
PSALM 37:7

Have you prayed and prayed and waited and waited, and still there is no manifestation? Are you tired of seeing nothing move? Are you just at the point of giving it all up? Perhaps you have not waited in the right way?

"With patience wait" (Romans 8:25). Patience takes away worry. He said He would come, and His promise is equal to His presence. Patience takes away your weeping. Why feel sad and despondent? He knows your need better than you do, and His purpose in waiting is to bring more glory out of it all. Patience takes away self-works. The work He desires is that you "believe" (John 6:29), and when you believe, you may then know that all is well. Patience takes away all want. Your desire for the thing you wish is perhaps stronger than your desire for the will of God to be fulfilled in its arrival.

Patience takes away all weakening. Instead of having the delaying time, a time of letting go, know that God is getting a larger supply ready and must get you ready too. Patience takes away all wobbling. "Made me stand upon my standing" (Daniel 8:18 margin). God's foundations are steady; and when His patience is within, we are steady while we wait. Patience gives worship. A praiseful patience, sometimes "long-suffering with joyfulness" (Colossians 1:11), is the best part of it all. "Let (all these phases of) patience have her perfect work" (James 1:4), while you wait, and you will find great enrichment.

from *Streams in the Desert*
by MRS. CHARLES E. COWMAN

LAID BACK

But the LORD is in his holy temple:
let all the earth keep silence before him.
HABAKKUK 2:20

Nicole tapped her toe and threw a magazine onto the windowsill. She'd read every magazine in the coronary unit's waiting room; rather, she had tried to read them. Nothing held her attention more than a few paragraphs. She stood up and stared out the window to the hospital parking lot one story below and wondered briefly what heartache hid in the cars streaming in and out. Did the drivers have a loved one lying in one of the hospital beds, hovering between life and death like her husband? Without realizing what she did, she began to pace between the window and the door to the hall. At the end of the hall, the nurses bustled in and out of their station. She walked down to see if they had an update on Gordon. They didn't.

"Mrs. Porter, how is your husband?"

Nicole looked around to see Dr. Prescott, the woman who had been on duty when Gordon's ambulance screeched into the emergency room five days ago. Was it only five days? It seemed like three weeks. How the time dragged. What was the date today? She couldn't think.

"It's still nip and tuck," Nicole told the woman. "The cardiologist won't commit to a prognosis."

"How are you coping with the stress?" Dr. Prescott put a sympathetic hand on her arm.

"By fidgeting, I guess." Nicole twisted her hands together. "What do you do with stress in a situation like this?"

"I quilt." Dr. Prescott gestured toward the tote she carried.

"Quilt? I wouldn't be able to concentrate on sewing. I can't even read a magazine article."

"The emergency room is the scene of a lot of tension. When I first started twelve-hour shifts there, I thought I'd go bonkers from the pressure of making the right split-second decisions, or I'd go mad from boredom when nothing happened for hours on end. Now I quilt between patients. It doesn't require much concentration, and it relaxes me. Tell you what I'll do. I keep a kit on hand ready to begin, pieces cut, and thread and needles assembled. I'll bring a simple one to you tomorrow and show you how to get started."

Dr. Prescott walked away before Nicole could protest.

The quilt the doctor arrived with in the morning was small and looked simple. It involved appliquéing six sunbonnet girls on muslin separated by strips of multicolored material that carried all the colors of the girls' dresses. Their location was already marked on the background fabric.

Reluctant to hurt Dr. Prescott's feelings by rejecting her kind gift, Nicole accepted the quilt and the instructions about how to begin. By noon, she had been allowed in to see her husband twice, and she had stitched down the hats and dresses of two of the girls. She didn't roam between the door and window, and she chattered about the project to her husband, describing the dolls in detail. She thought her husband's eyes showed interest. She traced his lips with one fingertip. Wasn't that a tiny smile?

Before the week was over, Nicole had finished the appliqué. Following Dr. Prescott's directions, she basted the front to the batting and the backing. She enjoyed quilting around the outline of the girls. By the time she had finished the top half of the quilt, she succeeded in making her stitches smaller and smaller and felt pleased with herself. A peace settled over her as she worked on her project. Dr. Prescott was right. Quilting soothed her. By the time Gordon had recovered enough to transfer to another hospital for physical therapy, she had finished the wall hanging. She went to the quilt shop and bought supplies and instructions to begin another one to occupy her time during the long waits for doctors and therapy.

When circumstances agitate us, we can go to God and ask Him to help us become still before Him. By becoming quiet before God, we hear Him better because our agitated and distracted mind gets out of the way. Once we convince ourselves God is not surprised by our situation, we can move on to realizing He is still in control, and we will gain peace. "Be still, and know that I am God" (Psalm 46:10).

from *The Quilt of Life*
by MARY TATEM

THE GOOD SHEPHERD

The LORD is my shepherd;
I shall not want.
PSALM 23:1

On their own, sheep will starve. They do not have enough sense to move on to greener pastures when their own is stripped of foliage. They will wander off into traps, standing helplessly while predators stalk them. Of all God's creatures, few are more helpless than sheep.

It is interesting that God calls us His sheep. We so often think that we have complete control over our lives, and yet we really are helpless. We need to admit our weaknesses. When we admit weakness, that is our strength, because then we understand our need for God. God will protect us, provide for us, guide us from place to place, and never leave us alone. He truly is the Good Shepherd; the best shepherd we could ever hope to find. We need a shepherd. Thank goodness we have the finest.

∞

Lord, I have difficulty admitting that I cannot do everything on my own. Help me to see that leaning on Your strength is not weakness at all, but power beyond measure. By Your wisdom I am saved. Amen.

from *Wisdom from the Psalms*

DRAWN TO OBEY

*For it is God which worketh in you both to will
and to do of his good pleasure.*
PHILIPPIANS 2:13

God's promise is that He will work in us to will as well as to do of His good pleasure. This means, of course, that He will take possession of our will, and work it for us; and that His suggestions will come to us, not so much commands from the outside as desires springing up within. They will originate in our will; we shall feel as though we desired to do so and so, not as though we must. And this makes it a service of perfect liberty; for it is always easy to do what we desire to do, let the accompanying circumstances be as difficult as they may. Every mother knows that she could secure perfect and easy obedience in her child if she could only get into that child's will and work it for him, making him want himself to do the things she willed he should. And this is what our Father, in the new dispensation, does for His children; He "writes his laws on our hearts and on our minds," so that our affection and our understanding embrace them, and we are drawn to obey instead of being driven to it.

from *The Christian's Secret of a Happy Life*
by HANNAH WHITALL SMITH

No Fear

Yea, though I walk through the valley of the shadow of death,
I will fear no evil: for thou art with me;
thy rod and thy staff they comfort me.
PSALM 23:4

To look at Bess and to listen to her talk, you would never have thought she was dying of cancer. She always had the same smile on her face and a kind word for everyone who came to see her. The other patients spent a lot of time with her, because her spirit seemed to be contagious. She ministered to her roommates by remaining cheerful and positive. Even the thought of death couldn't take Bess's dynamic humor from her.

The love of God can help us to endure many things. Circumstances that ordinarily knock us flat are as nothing when face-to-face with the power of God. Cry out to God in times of affliction, and He will comfort you and lift you above the fear of evil things. Truly, our help is in the Lord.

∞

There is nothing in this life, Lord, that I cannot face as long as You are with me. Amen.

from *Wisdom from the Psalms*

TRAVELING FARTHER

Casting down imaginations,
and every high thing that exalteth itself
against the knowledge of God,
and bringing into captivity every thought
to the obedience of Christ.
2 CORINTHIANS 10:5

I am constantly forgetting to recognize God's hand in the little, everyday trials of life, and instead of receiving them as from Him, find fault with the instruments by which He sends them. I can give up my child, my only brother, my darling mother without a word; but to receive every tiresome visitor as sent expressly and directly to weary me by the Master Himself; to meet every negligence on the part of the servants as His choice for me at the moment; to be satisfied and patient when my husband gets particularly absorbed in his books, because my Father sees that little discipline suitable for me at the time; all this I have not fully learned.

from *Stepping Heavenward*
by ELIZABETH PRENTISS

Opening the Door of Your Heart

I opened to my beloved;
but my beloved had withdrawn himself,
and was gone: my soul failed when he spake: I sought him,
but I could not find him; I called him,
but he gave me no answer.
Song of Solomon 5:6

Christ never forces any door open; He only comes in when we have opened the door. There is no power in hell or upon earth that can prevent us getting all God has for us. Only one person can do this, and that is you or I. He does not force anyone against his will to turn to Him and be saved. He does not force any child of His against his will to press on into His best.

If we would be refreshed by heavenly showers, we must take the steps that will bring us where they are falling. Though the droppings of God's mercy and grace, of His dealings and revelation, have their source in Him, and come from Him alone; though they are ever falling with copious blessings upon all who are where they can receive; only those who go where they are falling receive refreshment and have their prayers answered. We pray that the Holy Spirit may fully control us.

by CORA HARRIS MACILRAVY

TRUST AND WORRY

I will put my trust in him.
HEBREWS 2:13

Remember always that there are two things which are more utterly incompatible even than oil and water, and these two are trust and worry. Can you call it trust, when you have given the saving and keeping of your soul into the hands of the Lord, if day after day you are spending hours of anxious thought and questionings about the matter? When a believer really trusts anything, he ceases to worry about the thing he has trusted. And when he worries, it is a plain proof that he does not trust. Tested by this rule, how little real trust there is in the Church of Christ! No wonder our Lord asked the pathetic question, "When the Son of man cometh, shall he find faith on the earth?" (Luke 18:8). He will find plenty of work, a great deal of earnestness, and doubtless many consecrated hearts; but shall He find faith, the one thing He values more than all the rest? Every child of God, in his own case, will know how to answer this question. Should the answer, for any of you, be a sorrowful No, let me entreat you to let this be the last time for such an answer; and if you have ever known anything of the trustworthiness of our Lord, may you henceforth set to your seal that He is true, by the generous recklessness of your trust in Him!

from *The Christian's Secret of a Happy Life*
by HANNAH WHITALL SMITH

PEOPLE OF PRAISE

Thou preparest a table before me in the presence of
mine enemies: thou anointest my head with oil;
my cup runneth over.
PSALM 23:5

Some people never find satisfaction in the things they do have, but spend their entire lives wishing for things they don't have. They are never happy with where their lives are going; they feel empty in their relationships, and therefore they find it impossible to give thanks for the many blessings they have been given.

As Christians, we are people of praise. Every prayer we offer unto God should acknowledge the many wonderful things that He has done for us. Only a blind person can deny the beauty and splendor of this world. God gives good things to His children, and we should be thankful for all that we have.

∞

Lord, I cannot believe how much I have been given. Help open my
eyes to the many blessings that have been bestowed upon me. Make
me thankful, Lord. Amen.

from *Wisdom from the Psalms*

Knowing God's Precepts

Teach me Your statutes. Make me understand the way of
Your precepts, so I will meditate on Your wonders.
My soul weeps because of grief;
Strengthen me according to Your word.
Remove the false way from me,
and graciously grant me Your law.
Psalm 119:26–29 NASB

Have you ever felt as if you've reached the end of the road and the only choice ahead of you is a brick wall? When you reach that point, the only remedy is to look up! God is waiting for you to come to your senses.

In these verses, we learn the principles that can set things right. The first, revival, occurs when we truly "seek the Lord with all our hearts." Martin Luther, an Augustinian monk, recognized that the precepts he learned from studying the Scriptures didn't mesh with the teachings of the Roman Catholic Church. Therefore, in 1517, he openly stated his objections to these teachings by nailing his ninety-five "Theses" to the door of the church at Wittenberg. This began the revival which led to the formation of the Protestant church.

Confession of sin is the beginning of true hope. For when we acknowledge that we've failed, God can use our broken and contrite heart, through the Holy Spirit, to mold us anew.

Understand and walk in the way of the precepts by meditating on God's Word. If you're not participating in an in-depth Bible study, consider finding or starting one.

from *Daily Wisdom for Women*
by Carol Fitzpatrick

THROUGH LIFE'S CHANGES

But I trusted in thee, O LORD: I said,
Thou art my God. My times are in thy hand.
PSALM 31:14–15

Everything that is good and perfect comes from You, O Lord and Creator. How great are Your fullness and wonder. You shine on my life day and night with no shadow of turning away. Thank You for keeping the promises You gave in Your Word. You never forsake; You never fail. You are truth; You are life.

When I go through life's changes, I sometimes find myself getting way off base. But You snatch me from destructive situations. Thank You for being here. At times I can't see why things happen the way they do. But You know, and You are still here. Thank You for being patient with me. Thank You for how Your compassion and love never fail.

I'm growing in my walk with You. Because of all You teach me, I'm learning to give You my joys, my worries, my disappointments, my goals, and dreams. They are all in Your sure hands. Lord, You are first now in everything I do and plan.

What a comfort to know You will live forever and ever, and that I can always be with You. You have promised to always be my God, and keep me Your child. Through eternity, I cling to You, the Rock of my salvation. I shall never fear, for You are with me. You are first, last, always, my God and my dearest Friend.

from *When I'm on My Knees*
by ANITA CORRINE DONIHUE

Consent to Suffer

I delight to do thy will, O my God: yea,
thy law is within my heart.

PSALM 40:8

If you find, in the course of daily events, that your self-consecration was not perfect—that is, that your will revolts at His will—do not be discouraged, but fly to your Savior and stay in His presence till you obtain the spirit in which He cried in His hour of anguish, "Father, if thou be willing, remove this cup from me: nevertheless not my will, but thine, be done" (Luke 22:42). Every time you do this it will be easier to do it; every such consent to suffer will bring you nearer and nearer to Him, and in this nearness to Him you will find such peace, such blessed, sweet peace as will make your life infinitely happy, no matter what may be its mere outside conditions.

from *Stepping Heavenward*
by ELIZABETH PRENTISS

YOUR FAITH

And David said to Solomon his son,
Be strong and of good courage, and do it: fear not,
nor be dismayed: for the LORD God,
even my God, will be with thee.
1 CHRONICLES 28:20

Let your faith now lay hold of a new power in Christ. You have trusted Him as your dying Savior; now trust Him as your living Savior. Just as much as He came to deliver you from future punishment did He also come to deliver you from present bondage. Just as truly as He came to bear your stripes for you has He come to live your life for you. You are as utterly powerless in the one case as in the other. You could as easily have got yourself rid of your own sins, as you could now accomplish for yourself practical righteousness. Christ, and Christ only, must do both for you; and your part in both cases is simply to give the thing to Him to do, and then believe that He does it.

∞

Lord Jesus, I believe Thou art stronger than sin, and that Thou canst keep me, even me, in my extreme of weakness, from falling into its snares or yielding obedience to its commands. And, Lord, I am going to trust Thee to keep me. I have tried keeping myself, and have failed, and failed most grievously. I am absolutely helpless. So now I will trust Thee. I give myself to Thee. I keep back no reserves. Body, soul, and spirit, I present myself to Thee as a piece of clay, to be fashioned into anything Thy love and Thy wisdom shall choose.

from *The Christian's Secret of a Happy Life*
by HANNAH WHITALL SMITH

TRUSTING

O my God, I trust in thee: let me not be ashamed,
let not mine enemies triumph over me.
PSALM 25:2

Gail called herself a good Christian. She read her Bible, prayed daily, attended church every Sunday, and pitched in whenever her church needed her. God seemed to be a very real part of Gail's life, and yet, whenever her faith was put to the test, she seemed to give up. Her answer for everything was, "Well, God couldn't be bothered with me, I suppose." The truth was, Gail was afraid to put her full faith in God, for fear He might let her down. Her feelings of unworthiness blocked her from putting her trust totally in God.

Trust takes time. We need to practice putting our trust in the Lord, but when we do, we find a new confidence that He will be faithful to us. The more we trust, the more we are convinced that our trust is well placed. The key to trust is to try. Try putting your faith in the Lord, and watch wonderful things happen.

∽

Lord, assist me as I try to let go of my doubt and fear and put my trust in You. I sometimes become my own worst enemy, Father. Save me from myself. Amen.

from *Wisdom from the Psalms*

THE FATHER HAS BESTOWED A GREAT LOVE

See how great a love the Father has bestowed upon us,
that we should be called children of God; and such we are.
For this reason the world does not know us, because it did not
know Him. Beloved, now we are children of God,
and it has not appeared as yet what we shall be.
We know that, when He appears, we shall be like Him,
because we shall see Him just as He is.
And everyone who has this hope fixed on Him purifies himself,
just as He is pure.

1 JOHN 3:1–3 NASB

Have you ever looked into the mirror and thought, *I wish I had a new body?* Well, Christ has one reserved for you in heaven. That body is imperishable, undefiled, and will not fade away (1 Peter 1:3–4).

While we don't know when Jesus is coming again, we do know that our new bodies will coincide with this event. "When Christ, who is our life, is revealed, then you also will be revealed with Him in glory" (Colossians 3:4 NASB).

Yet the gift of our new bodies is only one aspect of the Father's incredible love for His children. His love prompts His children to purify themselves just as He is pure (1 John 3:3). They also abide in Him and practice righteousness (1 John 3:6–7), for they have been born of God (1 John 3:9; John 3:7).

from *Daily Wisdom for Women*
by CAROL FITZPATRICK

PREPARED FOR SERVICE

And as many as walk according to this rule, peace be on them,
and mercy, and upon the Israel of God.
GALATIANS 6:16

Lord, I have given my life to Thee,
And every day and hour is Thine—
What Thou appointest let them be;
Thy will is better, Lord, than mine.

A. WARNER

Begin at once; before you venture away from this quiet moment, ask your King to take you wholly into His service, and place all the hours of this day quite simply at His disposal, and ask Him to make and keep you ready to do just exactly what He appoints. Never mind about tomorrow; one day at a time is enough. Try it today, and see if it is not a day of strange, almost curious, peace, so sweet that you will be only too thankful, when tomorrow comes, to ask Him to take it also—till it will become a blessed habit to hold yourself simply and "wholly at Thy commandment for any manner of service." The "whatsoever" is not necessarily active work. It may be waiting (whether half an hour or half a lifetime), learning, suffering, sitting still. But shall we be less ready for these, if any of them are His appointments for today? Let us ask Him to prepare us for all that He is preparing for us.

FRANCES RIDLEY HAVERGAL

compiled by MARY W. TILESTON

DON'T PANIC!

The troubles of my heart are enlarged:
O bring thou me out of my distresses.
PSALM 25:17

Maggie was beside herself with anxiety. The last thing her boss had said to her was that she had to be in the office early the next morning. Her boss and the owner of the company wanted to "have a talk" with her about her "performance." What did that mean? Was it good or bad? Surely they would have told her, if it was good. Maggie just knew she was going to be fired.

Isn't it amazing what we can let our minds do to us? We blow things out of proportion and it causes such great suffering and distress. When we thrust ourselves into panic and fear, it is good to know that we can turn to the Lord, and He will be faithful to comfort us. Open yourself to His peace, and you will find new serenity.

∞

I let my mind get carried away sometimes, LORD. Please don't let me get too carried away. I need Your wisdom as an anchor when I set myself adrift in worry and fear. Be my salvation, Father. Amen.

from *Wisdom from the Psalms*

Rejoice in the Lord

Finally, my brethren, rejoice in the LORD.
PHILIPPIANS 3:1

The only thing that can bring unfailing joy to the soul is to understand and know God. This is only plain common sense. Everything for us depends upon what He is. He has created us, and put us in our present environment, and we are absolutely in His power. If He is good and kind, we shall be well cared for and happy; if He is cruel and wicked, we must necessarily be miserable. Just as the welfare of any possession depends upon the character and temper and knowledge of its owner, so does our welfare depend upon the character and temper and knowledge of God. The child of a drunken father can never find any lasting joy in its poor little possessions, for at any minute the wicked father may destroy them all. A good father would be infinitely more to the child than the most costly possessions. And, similarly, none of our possessions could be of the slightest worth to us, if we were under the dominion of a cruel and wicked God. Therefore, for us to have any lasting joy, we must come to the place where we understand and know "the Lord which exercises loving-kindness, judgment, and righteousness in the earth."

When all else is gone God is still left. Nothing changes Him. He is the same yesterday, today, and forever, and in Him is no variableness, neither shadow of turning. And the soul that finds its joy in Him alone, can suffer no wavering.

by HANNAH WHITALL SMITH

Letting Go

Therefore shall a man leave his father and his mother.
GENESIS 2:24

My first-grade daughter is still convinced I'm the most beautiful woman in the world. But a few mornings ago, my sixth-grader was embarrassed by my appearance.

She was already around the corner, waiting for the school bus, when I noticed her lunch bag sitting on the kitchen table. Without thinking twice, I grabbed it up, and dressed in my sweats, my hair still rumpled from my pillow, I dashed down the sidewalk, my old moccasins slipping and sliding on my feet. "Emily!" I shouted. "You forgot your lunch."

She threw a horrified look at me, and her eyes filled with tears. The other kids waiting for the bus whispered and giggled to each other. I glanced from them to my daughter, and suddenly I realized that I hardly looked my best. And I remembered once more what it felt like to be that age, when each small discrepancy in a person's appearance was fair game for ridicule and laughter.

Who cares? I wanted to tell her. *Don't let yourself be as petty as they are. Do you think I care what a bunch of twelve-year-olds thinks of me?*

But I cared what she thought of me. And it hurt to know that for the first time in her life, she was ashamed of me.

That day after school, she and I were especially nice to each other. I knew she had forgiven me for embarrassing her. And I forgave her for no longer thinking I was the most beautiful and perfect woman in the world. I guess I was really forgiving her for growing up.

from *Just the Girls*
by ELLYN SANNA

TO LEARN CHRIST

Looking unto Jesus the author and finisher of our faith.
HEBREWS 12:2

I have just been to see Mrs. Campbell. In answer to my routine lamentations, she took up a book and read me. . . "Wish always, and pray, that the will of God may be wholly fulfilled in you."

I said despondently, "If peace can only be found at the end of such hard roads, I am sure I shall always be miserable."

"Are you miserable now?" she asked.

"Yes, just now I am. I mean that I am in a disheartened mood, weary of going round and round in circles, committing the same sins, uttering the same confessions, and making no advance."

"My dear," she said after a time, "have you a perfectly distinct, settled view of what Christ is to the human soul?"

"I do not know. I understand, of course, more or less perfectly that my salvation depends on Him alone; it is His gift."

"But do you see with equal clearness that your sanctification must be as fully His gift as your salvation is?"

"No," I said after a little thought. "I have had a feeling that He has done His part and now I must do mine."

"My dear," she said with much tenderness and feeling, "then the first thing you have to do is to learn Christ."

"But how?"

"On your knees, my child, on your knees."

from *Stepping Heavenward*
by ELIZABETH PRENTISS

My Strength and Shield

The LORD is my strength and my shield;
my heart trusted in him, and I am helped:
therefore my heart greatly rejoiceth;
and with my song will I praise him.
PSALM 28:7

Karen wanted the semester to end so badly. She was tired and mentally exhausted. Nothing had seemed to go right. She supposed her grades would be fine, but grades meant very little when you felt so bad about all your classes. Better to be done with it and put it all behind. When the end did finally roll around, Karen felt as if the weight of the world had been lifted from her shoulders. Maybe things weren't so bad, after all.

If we put our faith in God, He will see us through the tough times, and we will emerge from our experiences renewed and wiser. He truly is our shield and strength. Rejoice in His great love for us, and lift your voice in praise.

∞

Lord, I can get through anything if I know that You are with me. Be close by my side, teaching me the way I should walk. Amen.

from *Wisdom from the Psalms*

THAT YE MAY KNOW

These things have I written unto you that believe
on the name of the Son of God;
that ye may know that ye have eternal life,
and that ye may believe on the name of the Son of God.
1 JOHN 5:13

Uncertainties are fatal to all true progress and are utterly destructive of comfort or peace. And yet it has somehow become the fashion among Christians to encourage uncertainties in the spiritual life, as being an indication of the truest form of piety. There is a great deal of longing and hoping among Christians, but there is not much knowing. And yet the whole Bible was written for the purpose of making us know. The object of a revelation is to reveal. If nothing has been revealed to us by the Bible beyond longings and hopes, it has failed its purpose. But I fear a large proportion of God's children never get beyond these hopes and longings. "I hope my sins will be forgiven someday"; "I hope I may be favored to reach heaven at last"; "I hope God loves me"; "I hope Christ died for me." These are samples of the style of much Christian testimony in the present day. Indeed, I have even known Christians who could never get further than to say, "I hope that I have a hope." If this word were used in the sense that the Bible always uses it, that is, in the sense of firm expectation, it might be all right; but in the use of it which I have described, there is so great an element of doubt that it does not amount to a Bible hope at all.

by HANNAH WHITALL SMITH

COMPLETE JOY

Fulfil ye my joy, that ye be likeminded, having the same love,
being of one accord, of one mind.
PHILIPPIANS 2:2

Nancy's excitement grew with each package the mailman brought to her door. Several months earlier, she suggested an ambitious project to her college friends now graduated and scattered to their individual lives. The group of girls had developed close friendships during their enrollment at Virginia Tech. For four years, they lived, played, and studied together. Their many opportunities to unite in worship seemed to cement their friendships more than any other activity.

Now, Susan, Nancy's college roommate, was planning her wedding. As a gift suggestion, Nancy asked each of the friends to make a quilt square which represented an aspect of their campus life together. Nancy undertook the job of putting the pieces together and doing the final quilting for the present. Every arrival of a finished contribution in the mail brought a smile. Nancy relished the creativity of her chums. One cross-stitched a map of Virginia and highlighted the location of the campus, every girl's hometown, and the bride's and groom's birthplaces. The square stenciled with penguins brought a giggle and an almost-forgotten memory of the bride's affection for the funny-looking birds. One of the patches was appliquéd with symbols of teaching since Susan had studied for that profession. The squares represented a nice selection of crafts. In addition to the appliqué, cross-stitch, and stenciling, there was candlewicking and freehand painting with appropriate sayings stitched upon them.

Nancy alternated the four-cornered fabric with heart appliqués of a pink printed fabric to create a cohesive design. For Nancy, the time she spent putting the finished quilt pieces together revived pleasant memories. She relished the love poured into each square as evidenced by the care taken for each design. The classmates were still "all in one accord," giving time and thought to make something which would bless their friend. The joys of friendship and shared activities, dreams, hopes, giggles, and tears were resurrected in the quilt.

As the deadline drew near, the pressure mounted, but the work remained a complete joy. Knowing her friends' eagerness to continue their friendship, in spite of separation, made the stitching worthwhile.

More than material possessions or even exciting experiences, our relationships bring us the most joy in life. Maintaining friendships requires effort. Relationships are cemented by shared experiences, laughter, dreams, and thoughts. The greatest joy of all comes from our relationship with God. Fellowship with God offers the highest kind of joy available to us on this earth. As human friendships are birthed with the investment of our time, energy, and thought, we develop our friendship with God in the same way. Find time to converse with our heavenly Father. Delve into His love letter to us, the Bible. Develop the habit of listening for His voice with your heart.

from *The Quilt of Life* by MARY TATEM

COMFORTER

And I will pray the Father,
and he shall give you another Comforter,
that he may abide with you for ever.

JOHN 14:16

Thank You, Father, for Your Holy Spirit, Your Comforter. What peace it gives me to know You are with me throughout my day. The world can't see Your comfort unless they choose to accept Jesus Christ as their Savior. Otherwise, they can never recognize Your sustaining power and grace.

I have so many questions to ask You about things I can't understand. I realize some answers may not come until I see You face-to-face. This is where I learn to trust You and depend upon Your Word. Guide me into truth and knowledge, so I can make right decisions. Let me learn from Your stories of old so I may grow in You.

I wonder what it was like that evening long ago when Your disciples hid in fear behind bolted doors, not knowing what to do next. Would I have been so fearful? I think so.

Past the bolted doors You came and stood before them. "Peace be with you!" You assured them.

I would have been thrilled and frightened at the same time if I could have seen Your hands and feet and side.

"Peace be with you," again You charged. "As the Father has sent me, so send I you." You breathed on them, and they received Your Comforter, Your Holy Spirit!

Breathe on me now, I pray. Fill me with Your Spirit. Grant me Your Comforter. Give me Your power so I may share the gospel in my life to everyone around me.

from *When I'm on My Knees*
by ANITA CORRINE DONIHUE

THE DOVE OF FAITH

Your heavenly Father knoweth.
MATTHEW 6:32

A visitor at a school for the deaf and dumb was writing questions on the blackboard for the children. By and by he wrote this sentence: "Why has God made me to hear and speak, and made you deaf and dumb?"

The awful sentence fell upon the little ones like a fierce blow in the face. They sat palsied before that dreadful "Why?" And then a little girl arose.

Her lip was trembling. Her eyes were swimming with tears. Straight to the board she walked, and, picking up the crayon, wrote with firm hand these precious words: "Even so, Father, for so it seemed good in thy sight!" (Matthew 11:26). What a reply! It reaches up and lays hold of an eternal truth upon which the maturest believer as well as the youngest child of God may alike securely rest—the truth that God is your Father.

Do you mean that? Do you really and fully believe that? When you do, then your dove of faith will no longer wander in weary unrest, but will settle down forever in its eternal resting place of peace. "Your Father!"

"I can still believe that a day comes for all of us, however far off it may be, when we shall understand; when these tragedies that now blacken and darken the very air of heaven for us, will sink into their places in a scheme so august, so magnificent, so joyful, that we shall laugh for wonder and delight."

ARTHUR CHRISTOPHER BACON

from *Streams in the Desert*
by MRS. CHARLES E. COWMAN

NOT YOUR OWN

*What? know ye not that your body is
the temple of the Holy Ghost which is in you,
which ye have of God,
and ye are not your own?
For ye are bought with a price:
therefore glorify God in your body,
and in your spirit, which are God's.*
1 CORINTHIANS 6:19–20

He has bought you with a price, and you are no longer your own.

"But," you may reply, "this is contrary to my nature. I love my own way. I desire ease and pleasure; I desire to go to heaven, but I want to be carried thither on a bed of flowers. Can I not give myself so far to God as to feel a sweet sense of peace with Him, and be sure of final salvation, and yet, to a certain extent, indulge and gratify myself? If I give myself entirely away to Him and lose all ownership in myself, He may deny me many things I greatly desire. He may make my life hard and wearisome, depriving me of all that now makes it agreeable."

But, I reply, this is no matter of parley and discussion; it is not optional with God's children whether they will pay Him a part of the price they owe Him and keep back the rest. He asks, and He has a right to ask, for all you have and all you are. And if you shrink from what is involved in such a surrender, you should fly to Him at once and never rest till He has conquered this secret disinclination to give to Him as freely and as fully as He has given to you.

from *Stepping Heavenward*
by ELIZABETH PRENTISS

APPROACH OF THE BRIDEGROOM

My beloved is like a roe or a young hart: behold,
he standeth behind our wall, he looketh forth at the windows,
shewing himself through the lattice.
SONG OF SOLOMON 2:9

When God sees us in danger of treasuring His gifts rather than Himself, or when He is preparing us for the walk of naked faith, into which very few of His children ever enter, He often withdraws from the open window, and we only see Him as He glances through the lattice. His apparent withdrawal brings a great distress, for in such dealing there is nothing between Him and us that has made Him withdraw. As our faith increases, we comfort ourselves with the assurance of God's faithfulness and unchangeableness; and we begin to discern Him as clearly through the lattice as we had before seen Him through the window.

But the Lord finally withdraws behind an apparent wall, which our eyes cannot pierce, though His eyes are ever upon us. Again we are distressed and dismayed, but as faith disperses the clouds of doubt and fear, He gives us "songs in the night." We are able to say: "I know Him whom I have believed." And the eye of faith is strengthened, that He begins to reveal Himself to our chastened vision; and we catch glimpses of Him through the lattice—passing visions of His beauty which we have never before beheld. If He hides Himself, we press on with our eyes more and more toward Him, and we endure as beholding Him who is invisible.

by CORA HARRIS MACILRAVY

Concerning Faith

But without faith it is impossible to please him:
for he that cometh to God must believe that he is,
and that he is a rewarder of them that diligently seek him.

Hebrews 11:6

The subject of faith is very generally misunderstood; for, in reality, faith is the simplest and plainest thing in the world, and the most easy of exercise.

Your idea of faith, I suppose, has been something like this. You have looked upon it as in some way a sort of thing —either a religious exercise of soul, or an inward, gracious disposition of heart; something tangible, in fact, which, when you have secured it, you can look at and rejoice over, and use as a passport to God's favor, or a coin with which to purchase His gifts. Now, faith, in fact, is not in the least like this. It is nothing at all tangible. It is simply believing God; and, like sight, it is nothing apart from its object. You might as well shut your eyes and look inside and see whether you have faith. You see something, and thus know that you have sight; you believe something, and thus know that you have faith. For as sight is only seeing, so faith is only believing. And as the only necessary thing about sight is that you see the thing as it is, so the only necessary thing about belief is that you believe the thing as it is. The virtue does not lie in your believing, but in the thing you believe. Your salvation comes, not because your faith saves you, but because it links you to the Savior who saves; and your believing is really nothing but the link.

from *The Christian's Secret of a Happy Life*
by Hannah Whitall Smith

Is Temptation Sin?

Blessed is the man that endureth temptation:
for when he is tried,
he shall receive the crown of life,
which the LORD hath promised to them that love him.
JAMES 1:12

Temptation cannot be sin; and the truth is, it is no more a sin to hear these whispers and suggestions of evil in our souls than it is for us to hear the wicked talk of bad men as we pass along the street. The sin comes, in either case, only by our stopping and joining in with them. If, when the wicked suggestions come, we turn from them at once, as we would from wicked talk, and pay no more attention to them than we would to the talk, we do not sin. But, if we carry them on our minds, and roll them under our tongues, and dwell on them with a half consent of our will to them as true, then we sin. We may be enticed by temptations a thousand times a day without sin, and we cannot help these encitings, and are not to blame for them. But if we begin to think that these encitings are actual sin on our part, then the battle is half lost already, and the sin can hardly fail to gain a complete victory.

by HANNAH WHITALL SMITH

THE GREAT COMMISSION

Go ye therefore, and teach all nations,
baptizing them in the name of the Father,
and of the Son, and of the Holy Ghost.
MATTHEW 28:19

We, as part of the church, must step forth and share the good news of what God has done for us with everyone and anyone who will listen. There is an urgency in this, for life here on earth is short. This is our commandment: to tell the world about the love of Jesus.

When you feel reserved or frightened about testifying of Jesus, think how you would feel if you inherited a million dollars. Could you keep quiet? Or would you shout for joy and tell all your friends the good news?

Christ paid our debt of sin and gave all who accept Him the most valuable gift of all: an abundant, joyful life on earth and eternal life with God in heaven. And it didn't cost a thing except submitting to His will and accepting His gift. Most incredible is that we can share this wonderful gift with those around us, so they may also receive Him. Our friends, our family, the hairdresser, the store clerk, our coworkers, the gas station attendant—the list goes on and on.

Stand up for Jesus. Use the Word of God for your guide. Help lead others to Christ. If you need assistance, call on a Christian friend or your pastor to help. But, you can also pray with someone all by yourself. What a thrill it is to watch a baby soul be born in the Lord!

from *When I'm Praising God*
by ANITA CORRINE DONIHUE

MORNING ON THE MOUNT

Come up in the morning. . .
and present thyself there to me
in the top of the mount.

EXODUS 34:2

The morning is the time fixed for my meeting with the Lord. The very word morning is as a cluster of rich grapes. Let us crush them, and drink the sacred wine. In the morning! Then God means me to be at my best in strength and hope. I have not to climb in my weakness. In the night I have buried yesterday's fatigue, and in the morning I take a new lease of energy.

My mother's habit was every day, immediately after breakfast, to withdraw for an hour to her own room, and to spend that hour in reading the Bible, in meditation and prayer. From that hour, as from a pure fountain, she drew the strength and sweetness which enabled her to fulfill all her duties, and to remain unruffled by the worries and pettinesses which are so often the trial of narrow neighborhoods. As I think of her life, and all it had to bear, I see the absolute triumph of Christian grace in the lovely ideal of a Christian lady. I never saw her temper disturbed; I never heard her speak one word of anger, of calumny, or of idle gossip; I never observed in her any sign of a single sentiment unbecoming to a soul which had drunk of the river of the water of life, and which had fed upon manna in the barren wilderness.

Give God the blossom of the day. Do not put Him off with faded leaves.

from *Streams in the Desert*
by MRS. CHARLES E. COWMAN

OUR ASSIGNED WORK

I will surely do thee good.
GENESIS 32:12

Thou know'st not what is good for thee,
But God doth know—
Let Him thy strong reliance be,
And rest thee so.

C. F. GELLERT

Let us be very careful of thinking, on the one hand, that we have no work assigned us to do, or, on the other hand, that what we have assigned to us is not the right thing for us. If ever we can say in our hearts to God, in reference to any daily duty, "This is not my place; I would choose something dearer; I am capable of something higher," we are guilty not only of rebellion, but of blasphemy. It is equivalent to saying, not only, "My heart revolts against Thy commands," but "Thy commands are unwise; Thine Almighty guidance is unskillful; Thine omniscient eye has mistaken the capacities of Thy creature; Thine infinite love is indifferent to the welfare of Thy child."

ELIZABETH CHARLES

compiled by MARY W. TILESTON

THE RECORD

He that believeth on the Son of God
hath the witness in himself:
he that believeth not God hath made him a liar;
because he believeth not the record that God gave of his Son.
And this is the record, that God hath given to us eternal life,
and this life is in his Son.
1 JOHN 5:10–11

The "record" God has given us of His Son has been given for the express purpose of making us know that in His Son we have eternal life. "This is the record," i.e., that God hath given to us eternal life in Christ, and whoever believes in Christ has this life; and of course, ought to know it. If we do not believe this record, and consequently do not know that we have eternal life, we are "making God a liar." These are solemn words, and yet, taking the commonsense view of things, what is a doubt of God's record but the making a liar of God? If I doubt the record of one of my friends, I do in effect make that friend a liar, although I may never dare to use the word.

The flood of doubt and questioning that so often overwhelms Christian hearts in these days was apparently never so much as conceived of in Bible times nor by Bible Christians, and consequently it was nowhere definitely provided against. The one uniform foundation upon which were based all commands and all exhortations, was the fact, taken for granted, that of course those to whom the commands and exhortations were addressed, knew that they were God's children, and that He was their Father.

by HANNAH WHITALL SMITH

THE DOORS TO PEACE

In your patience possess ye your souls.
LUKE 21:19

How do we find the peace and simplicity we crave in our lives? I think the answer lies in patience and prayer.

We all like to be busy, active, doing; we want to be in control of our lives. But sometimes circumstances force us to accept that we can *do* nothing. All we can do is be patient and pray.

But notice that life has to *force* us to this point. We speak as though patience and prayer were a sort of last resort for people who are too weak or too desperate to do anything else. We turn to prayer only when we are alone and undisturbed, and we practice patience only when we have to. After all, most of us would rather have what we want *now*, not later, and we'd rather be able to get it through our own efforts, rather than wait on God. And so we strive and strive, and our lives become more and more hectic and complicated.

In reality, though, patience and prayer should be our first resort, for they are the tap lines that enable us to find peace even in the midst of life's busyness and noise. They are the doors that lead us into God's peace. And they are the lessons that teach us simplicity.

from *Keep It Simple*
by ELLYN SANNA

The Bride Awakened

I have put off my coat; how shall I put it on?
I have washed my feet; how shall I defile them?
Song of Solomon 5:3

She does not see what it means to refuse to open the door to Him, for she is so nearly asleep, that her senses and discernment are clouded. Her own trouble, and what it will mean for her to rise and let Him in, are filling her mind, crowding out the apprehension of the sin she is committing. Her delay in opening the door does not look so heinous to her, for she knows that she loves Him; she would rejoice if He were within. She really desires to have Him within and longs to enter into that closer communion to which He is inviting and urging her.

Dear child of God, for what trifles have you and I repulsed our Lord when He has knocked upon our door and called us to rise up to higher ground? When He has called us to wait upon Him, and we found that it was hard to enter in, how quickly have we left our knees and gone away. We do not apprehend that He is calling us to get into the place where He can do something for us.

It only needs a few repulses through some trifle or selfish reason, and sleep will prevail. In the end, the bride loses what God is offering her and misses the blessing and the revelation that He is waiting to bring her. The best God has for her, she carelessly lets fall from her indolent and powerless fingers.

by Cora Harris MacIlravy

Yield, Trust, Obey

Neither yield ye your members as instruments
of unrighteousness unto sin:
but yield yourselves unto God.
ROMANS 6:13

To yield anything means simply to give that thing to the care and keeping of another. To yield ourselves to the Lord, therefore, is to give ourselves to Him, giving Him the entire possession and control of our whole being. It means to abandon ourselves, to take hands off of ourselves. The word consecration is often used to express this yielding, but I hardly think it is a good substitute. With many people, to consecrate themselves seems to convey the idea of doing something very self-sacrificing, and very good and grand; and it therefore admits of a subtle form of self-glorification. But "yielding" conveys a far more humbling idea; it implies helplessness and weakness, and the glorification of another rather than of ourselves.

Yielding is not the idea of sacrifice, in the sense we usually give to that word, namely, as of a great cross taken up; but it is the sense of surrender, of abandonment, of giving up the control and keeping and use of ourselves unto the Lord. To yield to God means to belong to God, and to belong to God means to have all His infinite power and infinite love engaged on our side. Therefore, when I invite you to yield yourselves to Him, I am inviting you to avail yourselves of an inexpressible and most amazing privilege.

by HANNAH WHITALL SMITH

DELIVERANCE

Many are the afflictions of the righteous:
but the LORD delivereth him out of them all.
PSALM 34:19

Carla couldn't believe how things were going in her life. She'd always thought Christians didn't have to face the same kinds of problems everyone else had. What good was being a Christian if your problems didn't let up? It seemed that since she became a Christian, everything had gotten worse. No matter how hard she prayed, she never felt God close at hand.

It is folly to believe that God liberates us from all discomfort and affliction. What He does do is give us the will and determination to go on, even in the face of tough times. He works within us to give us peace and strength and courage; those things necessary to get through life. We can be sure that our trials will not come to an end, but the love of God will see that we get through anything that comes our way.

∞

Lord, I sometimes feel I just can't go on. Please fill me with the strength I need, both of body and of character. Don't let me give up, but deliver me. Amen.

from *Wisdom from the Psalms*

DIFFICULTIES CONCERNING THE WILL

For that ye ought to say, If the LORD will,
we shall live, and do this, or that.
JAMES 4:15

There was a lady who had a besetting sin, which in her emotions she dearly loved, but which in her will she hated. Believing herself to be necessarily under the control of her emotions, she had fully supposed she was unable to conquer it, unless her emotions should first be changed. But she learned this secret concerning the will, and going to her closet she said, "Lord, Thou seest that with my emotions I love this sin, but in my real central self I hate it. Until now my emotions have had the mastery; but now I put my will into Thy hands, and give it up to Thy working. I will never again consent in my will to yield to this sin. Take possession of my will, and work in me to will and to do of Thy good pleasure."

Immediately she began to find deliverance. The Lord took possession of the will thus surrendered to Himself and began to work in her by His own power, so that His will in the matter gained the mastery over her emotions, and she found herself delivered, not by the power of an outward commandment, but by the inward power of the Spirit of God, "working in her that which was well pleasing in his sight."

from *The Christian's Secret of a Happy Life*
by HANNAH WHITALL SMITH

LIGHTHOUSE KEEPERS

Let your light so shine before men,
that they may see your good works,
and glorify your Father which is in heaven.
MATTHEW 5:16

Most lighthouse keepers have been men, but many women keepers also worked this lonely job. In the nineteenth century, the federal government made provision for widows of recently deceased lighthouse keepers, giving them first preference to fill their husbands' positions. One widow, Kate Walker, became the light keeper at Robbins Reef Lighthouse in New York Harbor after her husband's death. Over the years, she rescued more than fifty fishermen in distress. She raised her two sons alone and tended the lighthouse until she was seventy-three years old.

Our world is full of men and women who, in their own quiet ways, are as heroic as Kate Walker. These individuals shine the light of Christ over the world. They are beacons of hope that spread the gospel message: We no longer have to live in darkness, for the light of God has come to us in Christ.

∞

We thank You, Christ, for the light You shed into our lives. May we, too, be beacons of hope to the world around us.

from *A Beacon of Hope*
by ELLYN SANNA

NEVER ALONE

Plead my cause, O LORD, with them that strive with me:
fight against them that fight against me.
PSALM 35:1

We need friends and supporters. Jesus sent the disciples out two by two because He knew how important it was to have someone to share with and to support. Standing alone, we feel like our strength is limited, but with someone else by our side, new reserves of strength surface. Psychologically, we need confirmation that what we believe in is true. Just one other person can give us all the confirmation we need.

It is good to remember that our Lord strives along beside us, never leaving us, pleading our cause at every step. He understands us, loves us, and never turns away from us. Because of the mighty love of God, we can be assured that we are never alone.

∞

Lord, be with me this day. Support me in the things I desire to do, and help me to always follow the right path. Amen.

from *Wisdom from the Psalms*

The Meaning of Trouble

Thou hast turned for me my mourning into dancing:
thou hast put off my sackcloth,
and girded me with gladness.
PSALM 30:11; SEE ALSO ISAIAH 35:6–7

Many times in my life in practical affairs I have had my "mourning turned into dancing," because I have found that the trial I mourned was really a gateway into the good things I longed for. And I cannot help suspecting that this is far more often the case than we are inclined to think. I knew a man who had both his feet frozen off, and was thwarted in all his plans by the lameness that ensued. He thought his life was ruined and mourned with unspeakable anguish. But this very trial opened out for him another career which proved finally to be the thing of all others he would have chosen, and which brought him a success far beyond the wildest dreams of his early aspirations. His greatest trouble became his greatest triumph. Instances of this are innumerable. Every life has some.

Since we have so often experienced our deserts to be turned into the garden of the Lord, and have found fir trees and myrtle trees coming up where we thought there were only thorns and briers, the marvelous thing is that we should ever let ourselves be so utterly cast down and overwhelmed when fresh trouble comes. I think it would be a good exercise of soul for us to write out a little record for our own use of all the times when this marvelous transformation has happened in our experience. It might make us less ready to despair under our next trial.

by HANNAH WHITALL SMITH

THE COAT

He that hath two coats, let him impart to him that hath none.
LUKE 3:11

After Fran's older sister died, Fran donated most of her clothing to charity. One of the few items she kept was The Coat.

Just touching The Coat brought memories of Joy's laughing face. Fran wore The Coat after Joy died.

A year later, Fran thought of a teacher going through hard times. Would Susan feel insulted if she offered her the rest of Joy's clothing?

A startling thought came: *Give Susan Joy's coat.* "What?" she protested. *Susan needs it more than you do,* the small inner voice whispered.

"Offering Susan an old coat might hurt her feelings, Lord." A bright idea came. "How about a test? If I'm supposed to give Susan The Coat, help me find a replacement for. . ." (She named a ridiculously low figure.) A few hours later, she found a coat far below her stated limit.

That evening Susan dropped by Fran's house. Fran brought out two almost-new sweatshirts. "Can you use a few things?" Susan's face lit up, so Fran added, "There's one more thing." She took The Coat from a closet.

Susan swallowed hard and bowed her head.

When she looked up, her lips quivered. "For weeks I've been praying for a winter coat, but didn't know how it was possible."

May we always appreciate our blessings as much as Susan appreciated The Coat.

from *A Teacher's Heart*
by ANITA CORRINE DONIHUE and COLLEEN REECE

UNDER HIS WINGS

How excellent is thy lovingkindness, O God!
therefore the children of men put their trust
under the shadow of thy wings.

PSALM 36:7

The chicks scurried around as the rain began to fall. They had been out in the yard in front of the coop. When the storm hit, they flew into a panic. Carefully, but quickly, the mother hen gathered her chicks to herself, enfolding them in her wings.

Jesus used the same image to show His disciples how God would save His children in time of distress. We have no need to fear, for the Lord is watching over us, and He will pull us toward Himself during bad times. The love of God is beyond human comprehension. We need not understand it, only accept it.

∞

Father of all creation, You care for us in very special ways. We turn to You for comfort and security in a frightening time. Be with us always. Amen.

from *Wisdom from the Psalms*

DAILY BREAD

Thy words were found, and I did eat them;
and thy word was unto me the joy and rejoicing of mine heart:
for I am called by thy name, O LORD God of hosts.
JEREMIAH 15:16

Very few persons realize the effect of thought upon the condition of the soul, that it is in fact its food, the substance from which it evolves its strength and health and beauty, or upon which it may become weak and unhealthy and deformed. If we think low and corrupt thoughts, we bring diseases upon our soul, just as really as we bring diseases upon our body by eating corrupt and improper food. The man who thinks about self, feeds on self, just in proportion to the amount of thought he gives to self; and may at last become puffed up with self, and suffer from the dreadful disease of self-conceit and self-importance. On the other hand, if we think of Christ, we feed on Christ. We eat His flesh and blood practically, by filling our souls with believing thoughts of Him. He tells us this when He says, "It is the spirit that quickeneth; the flesh profiteth nothing: the words that I speak unto you, they are spirit, and they are life" (John 6:63). If we will take the words of God, that is, His revealed truth, into our lips and eat it; that is, if we will dwell upon His words and say them over and over to ourselves, and thoroughly take in and assimilate their meaning in a commonsense sort of way, we shall find that our soul-life is fed and nourished by them, and is made strong and vigorous in consequence.

by HANNAH WHITALL SMITH

DEPRESSION

The peace of God, which passeth all understanding.
PHILIPPIANS 4:7

My nights are sleepless again, dear Lord. Shadows creep around my room. I toss and turn in anguish. When I finally do sleep, I bolt up in bed, frightened that something or someone is after me.

I realize I need Your help more than ever. Life is too tough for me to handle. Lead me to people who can help. Open my mind to ways for me to overcome this terrible depression.

At times I am so distraught I can't even pray. Yet Your Holy Spirit knows my heart. I know You are lifting my needs to my heavenly Father in words that can never be expressed by any human. I take comfort in that.

Let me give my burdens all to You, my Lord. I must let You carry them for me. Most of all, help me be willing not to take them back.

I know You watch over me and will help me through this. I put my trust in You. I won't depend on my own understanding. I purpose to acknowledge You in every way and be alert to Your direction. Let me not worry. Help me do my best to solve each problem as it comes along and pray about everything, large and small. Here are my anxieties and my problems. I thank You for your answers, given according to Your will. You know my needs before I ask.

from *When I'm on My Knees*
by ANITA CORRINE DONIHUE

True Desires

Delight thyself also in the LORD;
and he shall give thee the desires of thine heart.
PSALM 37:4

I remember thinking, when I first became a Christian, how wonderful prayer would be. All I would have to do was let God know what I wanted, and He promised that I would have it. I began searching my life for the true desires of my heart, and was surprised to find that they weren't cars, money, or houses, but love, peace of mind, and happiness. The more I prayed, the more I became aware that the true desires of my heart were the desires of Jesus' own heart. They had been there all along, but I had never recognized them before.

Prayer is not a way for us to make ourselves wealthy and prosperous. The Christian's mind should be set on higher things. When we pray to the Lord, always remembering to say, "Thy will be done," we will find the truth of Christ squarely centered in our lives.

∞

There are few people I would rather spend my time with than You, Lord, though often I don't spend time with You as I should. Forgive me when I forget to turn to You. Make Your desires my desires. Amen.

from *Wisdom from the Psalms*

MATURITY IN THE LORD

*For unto the angels hath he not put in subjection
the world to come, whereof we speak.*
HEBREWS 2:5

I knew a lady who had entered into this life of faith with a great outpouring of the Spirit. She expected to be put forth immediately into the Lord's harvest field. Instead of this, almost at once her husband lost all his money, and she was shut up in her own house to attend to all sorts of domestic duties, with no time or strength left for any gospel work at all. She accepted the discipline. And the result was that, through this very training, He made her into a vessel "meet for the master's use, and prepared unto every good work" (2 Timothy 2:21).

Another lady, who had entered this life of faith under similar circumstances, was shut up with two peevish invalid children to nurse, and humor, and amuse all day long. Unlike the first one, this lady did not accept the training, and went back into a state of sad coldness and misery. She had understood her part of trusting to begin with, but she took herself out of the hands of the heavenly Potter, and the vessel was marred on the wheel.

The maturity of a Christian experience cannot be reached in a moment, but is the result of the work of God's Holy Spirit. And we cannot hope to reach this maturity in any way other than by yielding ourselves up, utterly and willingly, to His mighty working.

from *The Christian's Secret of a Happy Life*
by HANNAH WHITALL SMITH

Finding God in Everyday Life

He shall. . .gently lead those that are with young.
ISAIAH 40:11

I have made prayer too much of a luxury and have often inwardly chafed and fretted when the care of my children, at times, made it utterly impossible to leave them for private devotion—when they have been sick, for instance, or other like emergencies. I reasoned this way: "Here is a special demand on my patience, and I am naturally impatient. I must have time to go away and entreat the Lord to equip me for this conflict." But I see now that the simple act of cheerful acceptance of the duty imposed and the solace and support withdrawn would have united me more fully to Christ than the highest enjoyment of His presence in prayer could.

from *Stepping Heavenward*
by ELIZABETH PRENTISS

A WONDERFUL LIFE

My heart panteth, my strength faileth me:
as for the light of mine eyes, it also is gone from me.
PSALM 38:10

Emma was as old as the hills. She had mothered a dozen children, tended a hundred grandchildren, and no one knew how many great- and great-great grandchildren. She worked every day of the first ninety years of her life, then she decided to rest. In her one-hundred-and-third year, she lost her sight, and two years later she was confined to a wheelchair. For a while, she was resentful of losing her faculties, but in time she accepted it. After all, hadn't she lived more than a full life? Hadn't God given her more family than any one woman had a right to have? When all was said and done, Emma had had a wonderful life, and a few inconveniences at the end certainly weren't going to get her down.

We have two simple options when afflictions strike. We can moan about our fate and give up, or we can face it boldly and make the best of it. God grants us the power to become more than conquerors, if we will only choose to use it.

∞

Lord, I know there will be times when my strength fails and my will is drained. At those times, fill my heart with Your will and power. Make me a fighter, Lord. Amen.

from *Wisdom from the Psalms*

SAFE IN HIS HANDS

This then is the message which we have heard of him,
and declare unto you, that God is light,
and in him is no darkness at all.

1 JOHN 1:5

It is, of course, evident that everything in one's religious life depends upon the sort of God one worships. The character of the worshiper must necessarily be molded by the character of the object worshiped. If it is a cruel and revengeful God, or a selfish and unjust God, the worshiper will be cruel, and revengeful, and selfish, and unjust, also. If it is a loving, tender, forgiving, unselfish God, the worshiper will be loving, and tender, and forgiving, and unselfish, as well.

The poorer and more imperfect is one's conception of God, the more fervent and intense will be one's efforts to propitiate Him, and to put Him in a good humor; whereas on the other hand, the higher and truer is the knowledge of the goodness and unselfishness of God, the less anxiety, and fuss, and wrestling, and agonizing, will there be in one's worship.

I have discovered therefore that the statement of the fact that "God is good," is really, if we only understand it, a sufficient and entirely satisfactory assurance that our interests will be safe in His hands. Since He is good, He cannot fail to do His duty by us, and, since He is unselfish, He must necessarily consider our interests before His own. When once we are assured of this, there can be nothing left to fear.

by HANNAH WHITALL SMITH

A HUMBLE SPIRIT

When thou with rebukes dost correct man for iniquity,
thou makest his beauty to consume away like a moth:
surely every man is vanity.
PSALM 39:11

Connie was driving everyone crazy. All four of them had taken on one aspect of the project, and Connie had finished hers first. Now she was delighting in harassing the others for their slowness. Her taunting came to an abrupt end when their boss marched in, thew the report at Connie, pronounced it "unusable trash," and ordered her to do it again. With a flush of embarrassment, Connie returned to her desk to start over.

Every now and then, everyone needs to be reminded that he or she is no better than anyone else. Conceit is a killing vice in the Christian life. God created us all equal. His image rests equally with every human being. Sometimes God needs to bring us back to earth when we get too puffed up. Those who exalt themselves will be humbled, while those who humble themselves will be exalted.

∞

O Lord, do not let me think too much of myself. When I turn my attention inward, I lose sight of who You want me to be. Let me be honest and open with myself, and help me to find new ways to grow. Amen.

from *Wisdom from the Psalms*

Pray and Believe

When ye pray, believe.
MARK 11:24

When there is a matter that requires definite prayer, pray till you believe God, until with unfeigned lips you can thank Him for the answer. If the answer still tarries outwardly, do not pray for it in such a way that it is evident that you are not definitely believing for it. Such a prayer, in place of being a help, will be a hindrance; and when you are finished praying, you will find that your faith has weakened or has entirely gone. Prayers that pray us out of faith deny both God's promise in His Word and also His whisper "Yes," that He gave us in our hearts. Such prayers are but the expression of the unrest of one's heart, and unrest implies unbelief in reference to the answer to prayer. This prayer that prays ourselves out of faith frequently arises from centering our thoughts on the difficulty rather than on God's promise.

You will never learn faith in comfortable surroundings. God gives us the promises in a quiet hour; God seals our covenants with great and gracious words, then He steps back and waits to see how much we believe; then He lets the tempter come, and the test seems to contradict all that He has spoken. It is then that faith wins its crown. That is the time to look up through the storm, and among the trembling, frightened seamen cry, "I believe God that it shall be even as it was told me."

from *Streams in the Desert*
by MRS. CHARLES E. COWMAN

Sorrows and Holy Living

For godly sorrow worketh repentance to salvation
not to be repented of:
but the sorrow of the world worketh death.
2 Corinthians 7:10

Doesn't it seem hard when you think of the many there are in the world, that you should be singled out for such bereavement and loneliness?"

She replied with a smile:

"I am not singled out, dear. There are thousands of God's own dear children scattered over the world suffering far more than I do. And I do not think there are many persons in it who are happier than I am. I was bound to my God and Savior before I knew a sorrow, it is true. But it was by a chain of many links; and every link that dropped away brought me closer to Him, till at last, having nothing left, I was shut up to Him and learned fully what I had only learned partially, how soul-satisfying He is."

"You think, then," I said while my heart died within me, "that husband and children are obstacles in our way and hinder our getting nearer to Christ?"

"Oh no!" she cried. "God never gives us hindrances. On the contrary, He means, in making us wives and mothers, to put us into the very conditions of holy living."

from *Stepping Heavenward*
by Elizabeth Prentiss

SOLID GROUND

He brought me up also out of an horrible pit,
out of the miry clay, and set my feet upon a rock,
and established my goings.
PSALM 40:2

Gina held onto the branch for dear life. The floodwaters swirled around her, pulling at her, threatening to carry her off in the raging torrent. The pouring rain blinded her, and large clumps of mud kept bumping into her. Her arms ached and throbbed. The last of her strength gave out, but as she let the branch slip through her fingers, a strong hand gripped her wrist. Gina felt herself slide up onto the bank of the swollen river, and she spread herself out to feel the firm ground beneath her.

There are days that feel like a struggle for life. How wonderful it would be to have someone come along and lift us up out of the struggle. God can do that. His Spirit renews and strengthens us. Through the loving power of God, we are pulled out of the darkest pit and set upon solid ground.

∞

Lord, hear me as I call out to You. Whether my problems are huge or tiny, I find I need your help to get me through. Pull me up into Your loving arms, and surround me in Your love. Amen.

from *Wisdom from the Psalms*

Overcoming Your Doubts

Trust in the LORD with all thine heart;
and lean not unto thine own understanding.
PROVERBS 3:5

Do not give heed to your doubts for a moment. Turn from them with horror, as you would from blasphemy; for they are blasphemy. You cannot perhaps hinder the suggestions of doubt from coming to you any more than you can hinder the boys in the street from swearing as you go by; and consequently you are not sinning in the one case any more than in the other. But just as you can refuse to listen to the boys or join in their oaths, so can you also refuse to listen to the doubts or join in with them. They are not your doubts until you consent to them and adopt them as true.

Put your will in this matter over on the Lord's side, and trust Him to keep you from falling. Tell Him all about your utter weakness and your long-encouraged habits of doubt, and how helpless you are before it; and commit the whole battle to Him. Believe He is faithful, not because you feel it, or see it, but because He says He is. Believe it, whether you feel it or not. Cultivate a continuous habit of believing, and never let your faith waver for any [reason], however plausible it may be. The result will be that sooner or later you will come to know that it is true, and all doubts will vanish in the blaze of the glory of the absolute faithfulness of God!

from *The Christian's Secret of a Happy Life*
by HANNAH WHITALL SMITH

The Joy to Come

Surely goodness and love will follow me all the days of my life,
and I will dwell in the house of the LORD forever.

PSALM 23:6 NIV

The Christian life is definitely not an easy one. We face countless hardships, trials, and temptations. We juggle the demands of family, career, and church responsibilities. We fret about health and finances. We grieve over the loss of loved ones. All too easily, we become weary and disillusioned as we question our hope and purpose.

When daily burdens become overwhelming, I love to read Paul's second letter to the Corinthians. He reminds them not to lose heart when they have trials and persecutions. He encourages his fellow believers to fix their eyes on Jesus instead of the things of this world. Our troubles, he says, are "light and momentary" compared to the eternal glories to come (2 Corinthians 4:17 NIV).

As a mom, I need to take time to set aside worldly cares and focus on eternal joys. I like to envision the beautiful reunions in store for the believer. Wives will be reunited with husbands. Parents will joyfully embrace their children. Mothers will tenderly cradle little ones that were lost to them on earth. And we will all meet at Jesus' feet, our hungry eyes feasting on His awesome and precious face.

How wonderful to know that in Christ we have a solid hope and future! How comforting that, at this very moment, Jesus is preparing eternity for us. And how awesome that our Creator actually wants us to spend forever in His presence. Oh, what joy waits for us!

from *Time Out*
by LEIGH ANN THOMAS

PRAISE YOU BECAUSE OF. . .

*"Who of you by worrying can add
a single hour to his life?"*
MATTHEW 6:27 NIV

To whom or what could I compare You, O Lord? Can any begin to measure the waters with the palm of a hand as You can? Is there one who is able to know the breadth and height of the heavens or earth's contents? Where is one who can weigh and balance the mountains, the foothills? There is no one.

Who knows all the movements of God's Spirit other than You? Can any see what all Your plans are for our future? Does one person know the day of Your return? There is no one.

The earth, these tiny nations, are less than a drop in the bucket or a speck of dust in Your immense vision. So with all this, how are You mindful of me? How do you know me by name? My joys? My heart-cries? How is it that You love me?

I cannot fathom it, Father. I only know You are my everlasting God. You never grow faint or weary in caring for me. Your strength goes beyond all other means I depend upon. Even with all our technology, You are even greater. You control the balance of it all. Because of this, why should I fear?

from *When I'm Praising God*
by ANITA CORRINE DONIHUE

THE CROSS

God is our refuge and strength,
a very present help in trouble.
PSALM 46:1

The cross I wear around my neck is not there for show, nor is it the object of my worship. I would not be lost without it, though I do like it. I do not believe it has some mystical power, nor does it protect me. The cross that I wear reminds me of the great love that God has for me. Christ's gift of eternal life is made real to me each time I look down at the cross or feel it lightly resting on my chest. In difficult times, I look at the cross and feel warmth and comfort. From its gentle reminder I draw strength when I am weary, refuge when I need to rest. Whether I wear my cross or not, God is with me, but sometimes it is nice to have a small reminder.

∞

I run to You when I need rest, Lord. You take me in Your arms and protect me from the pressures of the day. In every time of trial, You are the source of my help. Thank You. Amen.

from *Wisdom from the Psalms*

Safe Stepping

Thy foot shall not stumble.
PROVERBS 3:23

Many a Christian says: "I shall be kept from falling at last; but, of course, I shall stumble continually by the way." But have ye not read this Scripture, "Thy foot shall not stumble"? And if we have only once read it, ought not the "of course" to be put over on the other side? for "hath he spoken, and shall he not make it good?" (Numbers 23:19). And the Scripture cannot be broken.

But as a matter of fact we do stumble, and though "[he] riseth up again," yet even the "just man falleth seven times." (Proverbs 24:16) Of course we do; and this is entirely accounted for by the other "of course." God gives us a promise, and, instead of humbly saying, "Be it unto me according to Thy word," we either altogether overlook or deliberately refuse to believe it; and then, "of course," we get no fulfillment of it. The measure of the promise is God's faithfulness; the measure of its realization is our faith. Perhaps we have not even cried, "Help thou mine unbelief" as to this promise, much less said, "Lord, I believe."

"But how can I keep from stumbling?" You cannot keep from stumbling at all; but He is "able to keep you from falling" (Jude 24), which in the Greek is strongly and distinctly "without stumbling." The least confidence in, or expectation from, yourself not only leads to inevitable stumbling, but is itself a grievous fall. But again we are met with the very promise we need to escape this snare: "For the LORD shall be thy confidence, and shall keep thy foot from being taken" (Proverbs 3:26).

by FRANCES RIDLEY HAVERGAL

ME!

I communed with mine own heart, saying,
Lo, I am come to great estate.
ECCLESIASTES 1:16

There is no subject more vital to an everyday religion than a clear understanding of the right relations of our own individuality to the rest of the world. To most people the greatest person in the universe is themselves. Their whole lives are made up of endless variations on the word ME.

Like Solomon in Ecclesiastes, we "commune with our own hearts" concerning our great possessions of various kinds, our wisdom, our knowledge, our righteousness, our good works; and we are profoundly impressed with their great value and importance; and naturally we desire to call the attention of those around us to their magnitude!

There is never any "profit" in it, but always a grievous loss, and it can never turn out to be anything but "vanity and vexation of spirit" (Ecclesiastes 1:14). Have we not all discovered something of this in our own experience? You have set your heart, perhaps, on procuring something for the benefit or pleasure of your own great big ME; but when you have secured it, this ungrateful ME has refused to be satisfied, and has turned away from what it has cost you so much to procure, in weariness and disgust. Never, under any circumstances, has it really in the end paid you to try and exalt your great exacting ME, for always, sooner or later, it has all proved to be "nothing but vanity and vexation of spirit."

by HANNAH WHITALL SMITH

SHARING THE GIFT

Behold, God is mine helper:
the LORD is with them that uphold my soul.
PSALM 54:4

M abel never walked alone. In her hand was an old leather
Bible, which she read from all the time. It was bulging
with papers and sayings and handcrafted bookmarks, and all
her favorite passages were underlined in red pencil. She
delighted in sitting down with someone and showing him all
the history she had tucked away in her holy book. Mabel was
never without her holy Book, never without her smile. Mabel
loved the Lord, and nothing gave her more pleasure than
sharing Him with the people she met.

∞

Help me to seek after You, Lord. In the morning and throughout the
day, give me reminders that You are with me. Remind me to tell
others of Your love, that I might share the great gift I have been
given. Amen.

from *Wisdom from the Psalms*

Becoming Who God Wants Me to Be

I will praise thee; for I am fearfully and wonderfully made:
marvellous are thy works;
and that my soul knoweth right well.
PSALM 139:14

God does not call me to fit a certain mold, nor does He want to press out a bunch of cookie-cutter Christians, each one exactly alike. No, when God created me, He made me a unique individual with particular gifts and abilities. This is my true self, and as I become this person that God intended, I find that *I am happier and more free. I am also more united with the Holy Spirit, able to take the place God calls me to in His kingdom.*

from *Stepping Heavenward*
by ELIZABETH PRENTISS

TAKE TIME

Evening, and morning, and at noon, will I pray,
and cry aloud: and he shall hear my voice.
PSALM 55:17

Table grace was originally intended to help people turn their attention to God. The meals we share are a gift from God, and He is to be thanked, but we are also to reflect on the many other good things we are given. By praying morning and noon and night, we cover our day with a knowledge of God's presence and abiding love. We should take every opportunity to sing praises to God for all that He has done. Take time to pray. Make time to share your life with God.

∞

Father, I get so busy that I sometimes forget to be as appreciative as I ought to be. Help me to be thankful and attentive to the many gifts You have given me. All through the day, I will praise You. Amen.

from *Wisdom from the Psalms*

THE LIFE DEFINED

Take my yoke upon you, and learn of me;
for I am meek and lowly in heart:
and ye shall find rest unto your souls.
MATTHEW 11:29

Most Christians are like a man who was toiling along the road, bending under a heavy burden, when a wagon overtook him, and the driver kindly offered to help him on his journey. He joyfully accepted the offer but when seated in the wagon, continued to bend beneath his burden, which he still kept on his shoulders. "Why do you not lay down your burden?" asked the kindhearted driver. "Oh!" replied the man, "I feel that it is almost too much to ask you to carry me, and I could not think of letting you carry my burden too." And so Christians, who have given themselves into the care and keeping of the Lord Jesus still continue to bend beneath the weight of their burdens, and often go weary and heavy-laden throughout the whole length of their journey.

When I speak of burdens, I mean everything that troubles us, whether spiritual or temporal.

I mean, first of all, ourselves. Our own daily living, our frames and feelings, our especial weaknesses and temptations, our peculiar temperaments, our inward affairs of every kind— these are the things that perplex and worry us more than anything else, and that bring us most frequently into bondage and darkness. In laying off your burdens, therefore, the first one you must get rid of is yourself.

from *The Christian's Secret of a Happy Life*
by HANNAH WHITALL SMITH

PURITY IN MARRIAGE

Keep thyself pure.
1 TIMOTHY 5:22

On their wedding day, the bride and groom do not usually show up in dirty old clothes. Instead, the groom wears a spotless tuxedo, and the bride is dressed in a new gown, a gown of white she has never worn before. This new, white clothing symbolizes purity.

The word purity comes from two word roots. One means "to clean" and the other means "fresh and green," like the new growing life of spring. So when the bride and groom face each other on their wedding day, clothed in newness and purity, they are symbolically cleaned of the past so that they can grow into the future.

The Greek word for purity also meant "fire"—and by the power of Christ's grace, husband and wife come to each other in complete purity, a purity that burns the past's tattered, stained old rags, leaving the bride and groom dressed in new wedding clothes that can last a lifetime.

from *Something Borrowed, Something Blue*
by ELLYN SANNA

LOVE ONE ANOTHER

But those that seek my soul, to destroy it,
shall go into the lower parts of the earth.
They shall fall by the sword:
they shall be a portion for foxes.
PSALM 63:9–10

Tracy couldn't believe the girls at school would be so cruel. She never did anything to any of them, but they were always finding some way to hurt her. It was all she could do to keep from telling them all off. Her mother told her to ignore them, but that was hard to do. Her mother also said that they would eventually have to pay for all the nasty things they did, but Tracy wished that day would come soon.

No one likes to be picked on. Some people love to spend their time making others unhappy. These people will have to answer to God for their actions. We are called to love one another and to look for ways to give one another encouragement. While the nasty people will answer in shame for their deeds, the kind will rejoice with Christ in heaven.

∞

Lord, Help me to shrug off the unkind words and actions of the people around me. Lift me above the hurts that come from unthinking and cruel people. Teach me to respond in love, no matter how I am treated. Amen.

from *Wisdom from the Psalms*

The Unselfishness of God

For God so loved the world,
that he gave his only begotten Son.
JOHN 3:16

On the flyleaf of my Bible I find the following words, taken from I know not where: "This generation has rediscovered the unselfishness of God."

If I am not mistaken, the generation before mine knew very little of the unselfishness of God; and, even of my own generation, there are I fear many good and earnest Christians who do not know it yet. Without putting it into such words as to shock themselves or others, many Christians still at the bottom look upon God as one of the most selfish, self-absorbed Beings in the universe, far more selfish than they could think it right to be themselves, intent only upon His own honor and glory, looking out continually that His own rights are never trampled on, and so absorbed in thoughts of Himself and of His own righteousness as to have no love or pity to spare for the poor sinners who have offended Him.

To discover that He is not the selfish Being we are so often apt to think Him, but is instead really and fundamentally unselfish, caring not at all for Himself, but only and always for us and for our welfare, is to have found the answer to every human question, and the cure for every human ill.

by HANNAH WHITALL SMITH

CASTING STONES

But God shall shoot at them with an arrow;
suddenly shall they be wounded.
PSALM 64:7

Jesus stood with a group of His followers. In the distance, a crowd appeared, pushing a naked woman along in front of them. They cast her down at the Lord's feet and said, "What should we do with this adulteress?" They hoped to trap Jesus into advising sin.

Aware of the trap, Jesus gazed deeply into the eyes of the people. He stooped down and scribbled in the dust. Abruptly, He stood back up and said, "The one among you who is without sin, let him cast the first stone." (See John 8:1–7.)

His answer struck like a bolt of lightning. Words of pure love and power exploded their conceit, and they were forced to look at the truth of God openly and honestly. The sin was not at issue. What mattered was forgiveness. The hateful crowd was shot through the heart by an arrow of God's goodness. Killed was the sin of unrighteous judging. Whenever we present sin as righteousness, God will expose it for what it is.

∞

Turn my darkness into light, O Lord, and guide me away from things that are sinful and wrong. Teach me to love my neighbors rather than judge them. Let me cast love and peace, instead of stones. Amen.

from *Wisdom from the Psalms*

Left Alone

*And Jacob was left alone; and there wrestled a man
with him until the breaking of the day.*
Genesis 32:24

Left alone! What different sensations those words conjure
up to each of us.

To some they spell loneliness and desolation, to others
rest and quiet. To be left alone without God would be too
awful for words, but to be left alone with Him is a foretaste
of heaven! If His followers spent more time alone with Him,
we would have spiritual giants again.

The greatest miracles of Elijah and Elisha took place
when they were alone with God. It was alone with God that
Jacob became a prince. Moses was by himself at the wilderness bush (Exodus 3:1–5). Cornelius was praying by himself
when the angel came to him (Acts 10:1–4). No one was with
Peter on the housetop, when he was instructed to go to the
Gentiles (Acts 10:9, 20). John the Baptist was alone in the
wilderness (Luke 1:80), and John the Beloved was alone in
Patmos, when nearest God (Revelation 1:9).

Covet to get alone with God. If we neglect it, we not only
rob ourselves, but others too, of blessing, since when we are
blessed we are able to pass on blessing to others. It may mean
less outside work; it must mean more depth and power, and
the consequence, too, will be "they saw no man, save Jesus
only" (Matthew 17:8).

To be alone with God in prayer cannot be overemphasized.

from *Streams in the Desert*
by Mrs. Charles E. Cowman

THE PEACE OF GOD'S PRESENCE

Martha, Martha, thou art careful and troubled
about many things: but one thing is needful:
and Mary hath chosen that good part,
which shall not be taken away from her.
LUKE 10:41–42

Looking for peace anywhere except in the presence of God is just a waste of our time and energy. God alone is the source of all true serenity. Brother Lawrence, a seventeenth-century monk, learned this secret well, as the following description indicates:

> *Even in the kitchen's hustle and bustle, he never forgot about God or lost his focus on heaven. He was never in a hurry, nor did he sit around doing nothing, but instead he did each thing as it needed doing, with an even, uninterrupted composure and tranquil spirit. "These busy times," he said, "are no different for me than prayer times. In my kitchen's noise and clatter, with several people all calling for different things, I possess God just as peacefully as if I were on my knees."*

May we all learn to keep our focus on heaven even in the midst of our hectic lives! Then we can combine a Mary's listening heart with Martha's busy responsibilities.

from *Keep It Simple*
by ELLYN SANNA

GROWING IN CHRIST

Consider the lilies how they grow.
LUKE 12:27

What we all need is to "consider the flowers of the field," and learn their secret. Grow, by all means, dear Christians; but grow, I beseech you, in God's way, which is the only effectual way. See to it that you are planted in grace, and then let the Divine Husbandman cultivate you in His own way and by His own means. Put yourselves out in the sunshine of His presence, and let the dew of heaven come down upon you, and see what will be the result. Leaves and flowers and fruit must surely come in their season; for your Husbandman is skillful, and He never fails in His harvesting. Only see to it that you oppose no hindrance to the shining of the Sun of Righteousness, or the falling of the dew from heaven. The thinnest covering may serve to keep off the sunshine and the dew, and the plant may wither, even where these are most abundant. And so also the slightest barrier between your soul and Christ may cause you to dwindle and fade, as a plant in a cellar or under a bushel. Keep the sky clear. Open wide every avenue of your being to receive the blessed influences your Divine Husbandman may bring to bear upon you. Bask in the sunshine of His love. Drink of the waters of His goodness. Keep your face upturned to Him as the flowers do to the sun. Look, and your soul shall live and grow.

from *The Christian's Secret of a Happy Life*
by HANNAH WHITALL SMITH

A Gorgeous Sight

And let the beauty of the LORD our God be upon us:
and establish thou the work of our hands upon us;
yea, the work of our hands establish thou it.

PSALM 90:17

Rosemarie could hardly take in the beauty of the quilt. She wouldn't argue with the judges who hung a large, blue, first-place ribbon prominently above the breathtaking work. A flourishing flower garden filled the wall hanging. Hundreds of flowers fashioned from tiny bits of fabric splashed across the width of the quilt. Each flower was identifiable and contained two or more colors which combined to make the flower appear almost real.

Awed by the intricate work, Rosemarie wondered how many hours it took to piece together such a masterpiece. The craftsmanship and artistry of the piece before her made her own quilt tops look like the work of a kindergarten student. Even the garden wall was sewn with each brick individually fashioned and nestled to the next one. Subtle color changes brought depth as the wall curved away. The breathtaking beauty lifted her mind off of her trials for the moment.

Beauty does that. It offers a tiny respite of pleasure in the midst of life's difficulties. It's never a waste of time to acquire the skills required to create a splash of beauty in a world full of trouble and evil. Beauty is the nature of God Himself. A lovely creation in any artistic form reminds us of the God who created the ones who perform the artwork. While Rosemarie looked at the magnificent creativity of a woman who was only a name on a quilt show label, she thought about the creativity of her Lord, who was the ultimate Master Craftsman of her life and of all the lives of her loved ones.

When Rosemarie came to the quilt show, her heart felt

heavy with concern over her five-month-old grandson who lay in a hospital, fighting for his life. If God Almighty could inspire and enable a woman to create such a gorgeous sight as the quilt which hung before her, He could inspire and enable the doctors and nurses who were searching for causes and cures to restore her grandson's health.

Beauty inspires us to look more closely at the God we love. Seeing the beauty of God helps us better understand the depth and breadth of His love. The more we know God, the more we see His beauty and the beauty He creates in our lives even in the midst of troubles we do not understand. We come to appreciate God for Himself beyond what He does for us. Psalm 27:4 tells us: "One thing have I desired of the LORD, that will I seek after; that I may dwell in the house of the LORD all the days of my life, to behold the beauty of the LORD, and to inquire in his temple."

from *The Quilt of Life*
by MARY TATEM

GOD'S JUSTICE

For promotion cometh neither from the east,
nor from the west, nor from the south.
But God is the judge:
he putteth down one, and setteth up another.
PSALM 75:6–7

Evelyn came from Charity Hill, the most expensive section of town. She had always received everything her heart desired, and she considered herself to be one of the finest people she knew. Jane came from Cheesebox, the poor side of town, so named because all the houses there looked like cardboard cheese boxes. She had never had much of anything special, and felt she really didn't deserve better, anyway. Both women worked for an ad agency that wanted a new production designer. Evelyn knew she would do well in the position. To her dismay, Jane did even better.

Things don't always work so well in real life. The rich often get richer while the poor sink lower. And yet, God has promised that in the end, justice will always carry the day. God knows every heart and every situation. He will set all things right, if we will only trust in His wisdom.

∞

Nothing I do, Lord, will increase Your love for me, but still I want to do all that I can. Search my heart and know that I do truly love You. Help me to show that love. Amen.

from *Wisdom from the Psalms*

ON OUR BEST BEHAVIOR

Thou hast proved mine heart;
thou hast visited me in the night;
thou hast tried me, and shalt find nothing;
I am purposed that my mouth shall not transgress.
PSALM 17:3

Being a teacher for thirty years teaches you an awful lot. Ann had seen just about every trick in the book. The minute her back was turned, children would try all kinds of things. Often she would leave the room for a few minutes, just to see who her problem children were going to be. She would return suddenly and catch them in all stages of misbehavior. There were the exceptions, of course. Some children sat quietly whether she was in the room or not. Those children were rare treasures, but they often helped her keep her sanity.

All of us behave differently when we think we're being watched. Usually, we are on our best behavior when we know that someone else is around. The funny thing is, somebody is always with us: God. Is God pleased when He sees the way we act when we're alone? It is a wise person who tries to live righteously all the time, both when others are with him or her as well as when he or she is alone. God will help us be the people we are meant to be, if only we will ask. No one is more deserving of our best behavior than God.

Lord, help me to give You my best, not my worst. Keep me ever mindful of your presence, and be proud of who I am becoming. Amen.

by HANNAH WHITALL SMITH

GOD'S VOICE

Be still, and know that I am God.
PSALM 46:10

How wonderful it is when God speaks to our hearts. He warns us of entrapments and consoles us in sadness. How satisfying to feel the warmth of His approval when we've done right.

Sometimes we get so busy we unknowingly tune God out, just like flipping the switch on the car radio. He wants us to stay in tune. Each time we listen carefully for His still small voice throughout the day, we experience joy and peace. Then we are thankful we listened. He helps us avoid a lot of mistakes and heartaches.

When we pray, we are tempted to whisper a quick prayer, jump up, and go about our duties. We assume God's power is with us. How can it be unless we have tuned in?

I've caught myself doing this. It isn't long until my life becomes like one of the old 78 rpm records with the hole not quite in the center. How confusing everything is. I have learned the hard way to pause a little longer after I've said my part in praying, to let God speak to me. The communication goes both ways. When we listen, it completes the glorious circle in our friendship and love.

The next time you pray, remember SAL: Stop, Acknowledge Him, and Listen. Then we can go and serve.

from *When I'm Praising God*
by ANITA CORRINE DONIHUE

WALKING WITH GOD:
WALKING IN LOVE

And walk in love, as Christ also hath loved us,
and hath given himself for us.
EPHESIANS 5:2

If I love God, I will give myself completely to Him, surrendering each person and thing in my life to His care. I do not need to be afraid to do this, though, as I would if God were a human being asking me to make this sort of surrender. God not only asks me to give everything to Him, but He has already given everything to me, including His own Son; His love and commitment to me are far greater than I can ever imagine. Loving Him requires me to totally abandon myself—but my life is completely safe in His hands.

from *Stepping Heavenward*
by ELIZABETH PRENTISS

THE CLOSURE OF FORGET-ME-NOTS

Love covereth. . .
PROVERBS 10:12

Follow the way of love.
1 CORINTHIANS 14:1 NIV

Rehearse your troubles to God only. Not long ago I read in a paper a bit of personal experience from a precious child of God, and it made such an impression upon me that I record it here. She wrote: "I found myself one midnight wholly sleepless as the surges of a cruel injustice swept over me, and the heart. Then I cried to God in an agony for the power to obey His injunction, 'Love covereth.'

"Immediately the Spirit began to work in me the power that brought about the forgetfulness.

"Mentally I dug a grave. Deliberately I threw up the earth until the excavation was deep.

"Sorrowfully I lowered into it the thing which wounded me. Quickly I shoveled in the clods.

"Over the mound I carefully laid the green sods. Then I covered it with the white roses and forget-me-nots, and quickly walked away.

"Sweet sleep came. The wound which had been so nearly deadly was healed without a scar, and I know not today what caused my grief."

from *Streams in the Desert*
by MRS. CHARLES E. COWMAN

Inspirational Library

Beautiful purse/pocket-size editions of Christian classics bound in flexible leatherette. These books make thoughtful gifts for everyone on your list, including yourself!

When I'm on My Knees The highly popular collection of devotional thoughts on prayer, especially for women.
Flexible Leatherette................ $4.97

The Bible Promise Book Over 1,000 promises from God's Word arranged by topic. What does God promise about matters like Anger, Illness, Jealousy, Love, Money, Old Age, and Mercy? Find out in this book!
Flexible Leatherette................ $3.97

*Daily Wisdom for Women*A daily devotional for women seeking biblical wisdom to apply to their lives. Scripture taken from the New American Standard Version of the Bible.
Flexible Leatherette................ $4.97

My Daily Prayer Journal Each page is dated and features a Scripture verse and ample room for you to record your thoughts, prayers, and praises. One page for each day of the year.
Flexible Leatherette................ $4.97

Available wherever books are sold.
Or order from:

Barbour Publishing, Inc.
P.O. Box 719
Uhrichsville, OH 44683
www.barbourbooks.com

If you order by mail, add $2.00 to your order for shipping.
Prices are subject to change without notice.